THE NEW
CROSS STITCH
SAMPLER BOOK

THE NEW
CROSS STITCH
SAMPLER BOOK

Helen Philipps

David & Charles

For David

Acknowledgements and thanks go to the Embroiderers' Guild Museum Collection for allowing the reproduction on page 9 of a detail of an English Band Sampler of 1680, photographed by Dudley Moss, and to the Fitzwilliam Museum, Cambridge for allowing the reproduction on page 8 of the English Sampler of 1767.

A DAVID & CHARLES BOOK

First published in the UK in 1999

Text and designs Copyright © Helen Philipps 1999
Photography and layout Copyright © David & Charles 1999

A catalogue record for this book is available from the British Library.

ISBN 0 7153 0797 5

Photography by David Johnson
Book design by Roger Daniels
Printed in Italy by LEGO SpA
for David & Charles
Brunel House Newton Abbot Devon

Page 2:
The cottages from the four seasonal samplers –
Spring Time, Summer Garden, Autumn Days and Winter's Tale

CONTENTS

Introduction 6
Designing and Planning a Sampler 10
In Prayse of the Needle 12

INTRODUCTION

Sampler making has a long tradition and is very popular today with many reproduction designs available in kit form and books. People stitch samplers for many reasons, to commemorate family events and occasions and to give as treasured gifts, creating heirlooms of the future. In this book of new samplers I have explored some of the elements that make historic samplers so attractive and enduring but have also introduced contemporary design elements into my work. I have explored subjects using traditional sampler layouts and have added many new design elements to create a fresh and modern look. For example the four seasonal samplers – Spring Time, Summer Garden, Autumn Days and Winter's Tale – have direct links with the historic spot samplers of previous centuries. They show how easily a theme can be developed and how samplers can be personalised or adapted. It is hoped that this will provide the inspiration for you to produce your own unique sampler.

The earliest known samplers originated in the late fifteenth century and were stitched generally as reference sources and later for alphabets and numbers to mark household linen. These samplers were long, narrow pieces of linen with the stitching in the form of bands of pattern and spot motifs, pulled work and drawn thread work, and were normally kept rolled up in a work basket, not put on display to be admired. The first book to refer to samplers was *A Booke of Curious and Strange Inventions called the first part of Needleworkes*, published by William Barley in 1596.

By the seventeenth century wonderfully creative samplers were being stitched, both quirky and original. The embroidery technique known as stumpwork was very popular at this time and though not actually used on samplers, its charm and subject matter influenced sampler design. Stumpwork can still be seen in museums, showing the characteristic little figures and animals padded or worked over wooden 'stumps' to look three-dimensional, with texture created by stitchery and the addition of sequins, beads

and so on. The decorative qualities of these designs can be seen in samplers of this period and they have a delightfully detailed but naïve appearance. The Pastoral Sampler on page 20 has some of its design roots in this idea and my use of buttons and charms, for example in the Spring Time Sampler, echoes the style of these early stumpwork designs.

In 1631 a book called *The Needle's Excellency* was compiled by John Taylor, comprising many patterns for the needleworker and accompanied by rhyming couplets. One of these poems inspired my sampler In Prayse of the Needle. Another important pattern book published in 1624 was *A Scholehouse for the Needle*, which was very popular for its designs of flowers, birds and fishes which were used as spot motifs. The seventeenth century embroiderer loved these motifs and worked others like lions, deer, rabbits and tiny ones to fill gaps, like beetles, flies and caterpillars.

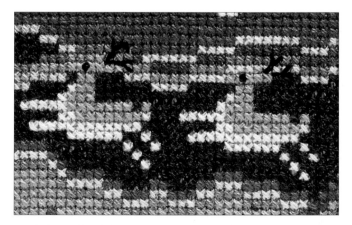

A stitching detail from the Pastoral Sampler (page 20)

In those days school children were taught to sew as one of the basic skills, and samplers were a good way for them to learn. In the mid-1600s, school samplers began to feature moral and religious inscriptions and often included the stitcher's name, age and date and sometimes historical or personal events. In America, the style of samplers was very similar though later

Right: *In Prayse of the Needle (instructions page 12)*

IN PRAYSE OF THE NEEDLE

Flowers, Plants and Fishes,

Beasts, Birds, Flies and Bees,

Hills, Dales, Plaines, Pastures,

Skies, Seas, Rivers, Trees.

There's nothing near at hand
or farthest sought
But with the Needle may be
shaped and wrought.
xxxxxxxxxxxxxxxxxxx John Taylor 1631

samplers bloomed into much more interesting and original designs.

By the eighteenth century the more familiar sampler layout was evolving as borders began to appear, made up of stylised flowers and leaves. Favourite motifs at this time were birds, crowns and hearts. When school pupils reached the part of their sampler where they could stitch a representation of their home, the creativity and imagination displayed in their pictorial images lifts even the most stereotyped samplers into an appealing art form.

Verses celebrating righteousness and obedience to parents were popular and samplers of this time often contained religious scenes and biblical quotations. The sense of doom at the high rate of child mortality was never far away and was expressed in such verses as this one, which I always find rather haunting when coupled with the name of its maker:

> *Lord give me wisdom to direct my ways,*
> *I beg not riches nor yet length of days.*
> *My life is a flower, the time it hath to last*
> *Is mixed with frost and shook at every blast.*

A stitching detail from the Candleford Hall Sampler (page 113)

Samplers displayed great variety at this time. There were samplers worked of maps and samplers in hollie point, darning, whitework and blackwork. In modern samplers similar textures can be created by using applied lace such as the Valentine Sampler on page 24. Blackwork too is increasing in popularity as more

modern designs are being produced for it. The striking imagery of the Candleford Hall Sampler on page 113 owes much to its blackwork border.

In America many stunning pictorial samplers were being produced, featuring buildings, ships, people, animals and farms, often with wonderfully detailed borders which became pictures in themselves. I have used this idea in the animal-filled border for the Red Fox Farm Sampler on page 90.

By the nineteenth century, however, samplers had become merely school exercises, often worked from books containing motifs which were reproduced many times. Children in orphanages produced samplers – usually in red thread on light linen – of alphabets and numbers, row upon row, as practice for marking household linen when they went into service in large establishments. The Victorians still produced religious samplers with some pious verses and many mourning

A well-balanced design featuring many plant and flower motifs by Ann Smith, 1767

samplers were worked during this era. Although the Victorian interest in all kinds of crafts increased, sadly the interest in making samplers began to decrease. It wasn't until the twentieth century that it revived, that antique samplers became immensely collectible and sampler making became popular again.

As you can see by the designs in this book, I have found sampler making and its rich history to be a continual source of inspiration. I have drawn on the style and layout of traditional pieces while at the same time introducing a fresh, contemporary feel, particularly by the use of modern threads, buttons and charms. The samplers and their spin-off projects have been designed to show how easy it is to adapt or create a sampler of your own and I'm sure you will find the process as enjoyable as I do.

Stitching the Designs

The following are useful general points about using this book and stitching the designs.

Samplers and Spin-off Projects There are 23 main samplers plus over fifty spin-off projects derived from these. In the majority of cases the spin-offs projects share the chart and key of the main projects and are intended to give you further stitching ideas, showing how flexible the designs are. Many of the spin-offs have stepped instructions while a few are explained in a more concise way.

Decorative Buttons and Charms Many of the projects use decorative buttons and charms which form part of the design. If you wish these can be replaced by stitching the charted motif or substituting a different motif from another chart in the book. The list of suppliers on page 127 gives details of where these buttons and charms can be obtained.

Materials Lists These are at the start of each project and give details of what you will need to complete the work. Some general supplies will be needed, such as a selection of blunt-ended or tapestry needles for the embroidery, mainly size 26. In some cases a beading

needle may be required for attaching seed beads. Sewing needles and sewing cottons to match the relevant project will also be needed for sewing up projects and attaching buttons etc.

Working Methods I prefer to work outwards from the centre of the fabric. To find the centre, fold the fabric in half and then half again and work outwards from here. When working on Aida or linen bands, start from the centre and work first along one side and then the other. I always work in the hand but you may prefer to keep your work taut by the use of an embroidery hoop or frame. There are many on the market.

Detail of an English Band Sampler, 1680

Lettering Library This can be found on page 119 and is intended to provide a range of additional alphabets which you can use to adapt or personalise the projects or design your own samplers.

Techniques and Stitch Library To avoid repetition within the actual projects, these sections of the book (pages 123–126), give you details of the various techniques and stitches required to complete any project.

DESIGNING AND PLANNING A SAMPLER

Finding Ideas and Creating a Design   *Finding ideas is the first part of the design process for me and visual stimuli are vital. My ideas come from many sources and I have been collecting interesting things for years – postcards, old china, bits of fabric, antiques, embroidery, samplers, painted furniture, gift boxes and reference books. I keep scrapbooks of cuttings from magazines, and record design ideas in a notebook, with a little sketch and perhaps colour suggestions too.*

I usually begin with a rough idea that I may sketch out, developing this as I stitch. Once I have decided what the sampler is to be about, I choose fabric that will suit it. For example, with the Seashell Cottage Sampler I began with the seaside colours of blue, aqua and sand, on white linen to create a feeling of freshness. I find it best to choose a generous selection of relevant thread colours and then select individual ones as I stitch, seeing which work best together. Unused ones can go into stock. I then look at reference books or my own photographs and drawings of the subject matter to find images I can stitch to 'tell the story'. In Seashell Cottage I used traditional images of the sea, sand, seagulls, Cornish cottages and shells.

My samplers may be directly inspired by historical sources and antiques. Candleford Hall took its inspiration from visiting old, dark, wintry Elizabethan houses. For this sampler I chose a dark linen, blackwork patterns (which were like the patterns on the architecture), silver thread (suggesting pewter), symbols of time passing (like the candle burning down), and a quotation chosen to tie in. Another source of inspiration for me is the written word. Some writers and poets create wonderful word pictures to inspire a drawing or design. The In Prayse of the Needle Sampler evolved from a poem.

Drawing a Design   *Once I have developed the basic idea of the sampler, what it is to be about, I sometimes make sketches of the design elements and layout. Mostly I prefer to stitch directly onto the fabric. If I am using an alphabet in the design I always work that out on graph paper first so I can position it correctly, and the same goes for verses, names and dates. You could design this way or work it out on graph paper first if you do not feel confident enough to evolve it freehand. There are various design aids that you may find useful when designing a sampler and these are described below,*

but the most important thing to remember, I believe, is to enjoy the process of designing and stitching. Choose subjects you really like and colours you feel happy with and if your heart is in it, it will show through in the finished piece.

Using Tracing and Graph Paper

Tracing paper is invaluable for copying motifs and patterns to include in your sampler and a limitless supply of images are available.

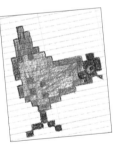

Tracing paper can also provide mirror images of a pattern or motif. Graph paper allows you to translate your design into chart form ready for stitching. It is also a practical way of assembling a complete design – each element can be charted on graph paper, coloured in and individually cut out. These separate elements can then be positioned on a master graph sheet, using temporary adhesive. Tracing graph paper is also available.

Using Photocopiers   Modern photocopiers with their facility for enlarging and reducing images are invaluable for experimenting with individual elements in a design, allowing you to manipulate the overall look and balance of a sampler.

Using Coloured Pencils and Pens   These are available in a large range of colours nowadays and

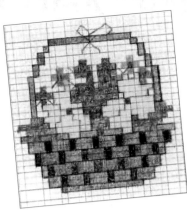

are extremely useful, allowing you to create charted motifs, colouring them according to your preference. You can experiment with an overall design by charting and colouring individual elements, cutting them out and pasting them onto a master sheet, as previously described.

Using Temporary Adhesives   Spray adhesives such as Spray Mount are very useful in the design process as they allow you to temporarily position the individual elements of your design (as described above) on a master graph sheet. Your overall design can then be studied and 'tinkered' with until you are happy. The whole thing can then be charted out in full, or you could begin stitching if you have the confidence.

Charting Names and Dates   You can personalise your work by adding a name and date or changing those on the samplers in this book. Using the alphabets and numerals provided, work out your details in pencil on graph paper, adjusting the space between the letters and numbers as necessary. Count the number of squares used vertically and horizontally and position the lettering centrally in the appropriate place on your chart or fabric. (See also page 24.) The Lettering Library on page 119 will help you choose your own lettering.

Charting Your Own Designs   It is easy to chart any element. If necessary, enlarge or reduce your chosen image on a photocopier. Place a piece of tracing graph paper the same count as the fabric you're working on over the design. Trace the design onto the graph paper, squaring up and eliminating any unnecessary details, then colour in.

IN PRAYSE OF THE NEEDLE

When I first read the poem featured in this sampler, published in
The Needle's Excellency by John Taylor in 1631, I was impressed by the
freshness of its message to stitchers today. The poem describes
the versatility of needlework so aptly and highlights its importance in
history. I visualised it as a band sampler at once (see photograph
on page 7), with an illustration for each image and appropriate charms
to add a further dimension. The sampler has been deliberately
designed to be lively, with a great variety of images and ideas, much
as traditional samplers would have been.

> **Finished size: 5¼ x 10¼in (13 x 26cm)**
> **Stitch count: 130 x 73**

- ◆ 11 x 20in (28 x 51cm) 14 count Rustico in oatmeal
- ◆ DMC stranded cottons as listed in the key
- ◆ Madeira Glamour thread, light silver (9804)
- ◆ Size 26 tapestry needle
- ◆ Gold-coloured charms (optional) – starfish, anchor
  and stork scissors (see Suppliers page 127)

1 Find the centre of the fabric and begin stitching
here over two fabric threads following the chart, using
two strands of thread for the cross stitch and two for
the lettering except 'John Taylor 1631'. Use one strand
for this and all backstitch, outlining and French knots.
Use an embroidery frame if you wish.

2 When the stitching is complete, use matching
thread to sew on the charms if you have chosen to
use them. The black dots on the chart indicate their
positions.

3 Press your embroidery carefully, avoiding any
charms you have used and then frame the work
(see Techniques page 125).

TIP

When using metallic thread cut shorter
lengths than usual as this will prevent the
thread from tangling.

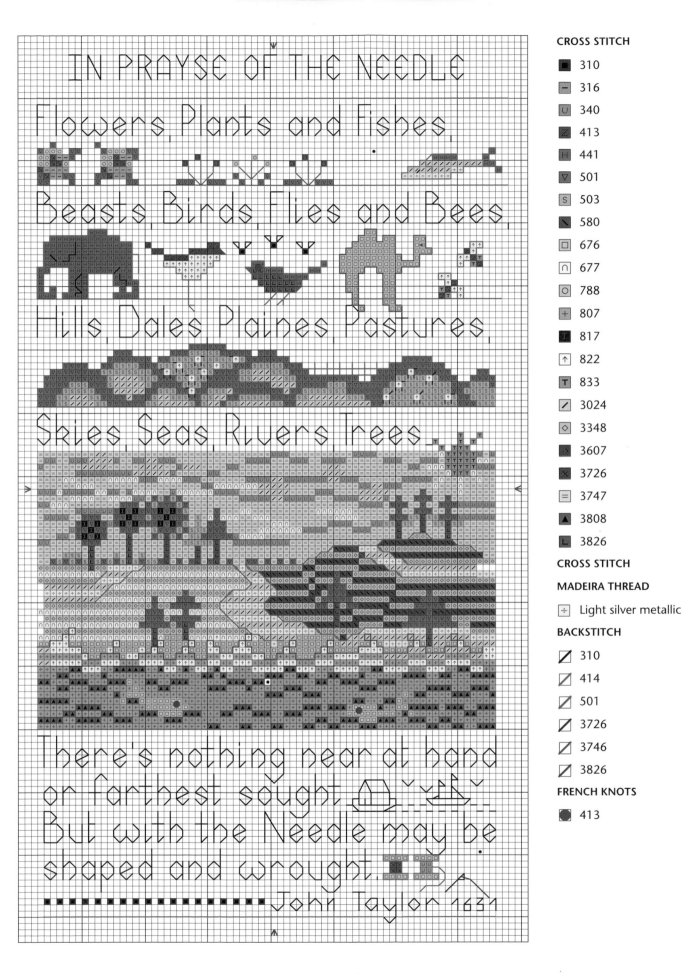

CROSS STITCH

- ■ 310
- − 316
- U 340
- ◪ 413
- H 441
- ▽ 501
- S 503
- ◣ 580
- □ 676
- ∩ 677
- ○ 788
- + 807
- ▦ 817
- ↑ 822
- T 833
- ╱ 3024
- ◇ 3348
- ▨ 3607
- ⊠ 3726
- = 3747
- ▲ 3808
- L 3826

CROSS STITCH

MADEIRA THREAD

- ÷ Light silver metallic

BACKSTITCH

- ╱ 310
- ╱ 414
- ╱ 501
- ╱ 3726
- ╱ 3746
- ╱ 3826

FRENCH KNOTS

- ● 413

SPRING TIM

Spring never did forget to bless
the year with broidered loveliness

Speedwell Cottage

NARCISSI

DAFFODILS

SEEDS

Spring is the busiest
time for the gardener

Spring Time

This sampler was designed as a celebration of spring, using motifs which epitomise that season for me, including daffodils, primroses, violets and daisies, Easter eggs, birds, nests and rabbits – all stitched in fresh spring colours. The layout of this sampler was inspired by traditional spot samplers where many different motifs are collected together, often surrounded by a unifying border. The sampler inspired many ideas for smaller projects, some of which follow on from this main sampler.

> **Finished size: 13½ x 10½in (34 x 26cm)**
> **Stitch count: 148 x 193**

- ◆ 16 x 18in (41 x 46cm) 28 count linen in white
- ◆ DMC stranded cottons as listed in the key
- ◆ Size 26 tapestry needle
- ◆ Mill Hill buttons (optional) – yellow bird-house, white bird-house, pansy, daisy, daffodil and tulip markers (see Suppliers page 127)

1 Find the centre of the fabric and begin stitching here over two threads of linen following the chart on pages 18/19, using two strands of thread for the cross stitch and one for the backstitch, outlining and French knots. Use an embroidery frame if you wish. When using space-dyed threads first cut up the thread into light and dark sections so you can recreate similar effects, like the shading on the tulip leaves. Use the Lettering Library to stitch the date and initials.

2 When the stitching is complete, use matching thread to sew on the decorative buttons if you have chosen to use them, or alternatively stitch motifs from the chart in their place.

3 Press the sampler carefully, avoiding any buttons used and then frame (see Techniques page 125).

EASTER GIFT BOX

This pretty box can be filled with chocolate eggs or gifts. It is made up of five panels, the base being unstitched. The primrose motifs are from the Spring Time Sampler – two in yellow and two in purple.

Finished size: 3½in (9cm) high x 3½in (9cm) wide

- ◆ **11 x 14in (28 x 36cm) sheet of plastic canvas 10 holes per inch (2.5cm)**
- ◆ **DMC stranded cottons from main key, plus five skeins of white (DMC B5200) for the background**
- ◆ **Strong darning needle**
- ◆ **14in (35.5cm) square of white felt**
- ◆ **Copydex glue**
- ◆ **3¼yd (3m) narrow yellow ribbon**

1 Cut four 3½in (9cm) squares of plastic canvas, trimming the edges. Stitch the first primrose in the centre of a panel following the main chart, using two strands and the yellow colourway (725 and 445).

2 Using two strands of pale pink (3609), cross stitch a border line round the panel, two bars in from the outer edge. Stitch a second line one bar further in using dark pink (3608). Fill in the background using two strands of white.

3 Stitch another panel to match. Then stitch two panels using the purple colourway for the flowers (725 and 522), pinks (3609 and 3608) for the border and white for the background.

4 Oversew the edges of each panel with six threads of white to bind. Cut four pieces of white felt the same size as the panels and glue to the back of each. Cut a piece of plastic canvas to fit the bottom of the box and glue felt on both sides of this.

5 When all the panels are dry, join the box together using a darning needle and cross stitch in four strands of white. Sew one side panel to the base then the other panels and finally join the vertical sides.

6 Glue ribbon along the top edges of the box, with small yellow ribbon bows in the corners.

TULIP AND VIOLET PICTURES

Follow the Spring Time chart on pages 18 and 19 and work on a 6 x 8in (15 x 20cm) piece of white 28 count Cashel linen for the tulip and a 4in (10cm) square piece for the violet. Work over two threads using two strands for the cross stitch and tulip stem and one for backstitch outlining and roots. Iron Vilene onto the back, trim, then frame.

EASTER CAKE BAND

Follow the Spring Time chart and stitch on a 32in (81cm) length of 2in wide white Aida band using cross stitch and two strands repeating the design three times. When complete, make a small turning at each end of the band and sew on Velcro to fasten.

EASTER HANGING DECORATIONS

Follow the Spring Time chart and stitch on an 11 x 14in (28 x 36cm) sheet of plastic canvas 10 holes per inch (2.5cm) using cross stitch and three strands. After stitching, cut out from the plastic canvas leaving one row of canvas all round. Oversew with half cross stitches in a matching colour. Using Copydex, glue a length of matching ribbon to the back, then glue matching felt on the back and trim when dry.

Right: *A selection of attractive projects using motifs from the Spring Time Sampler*

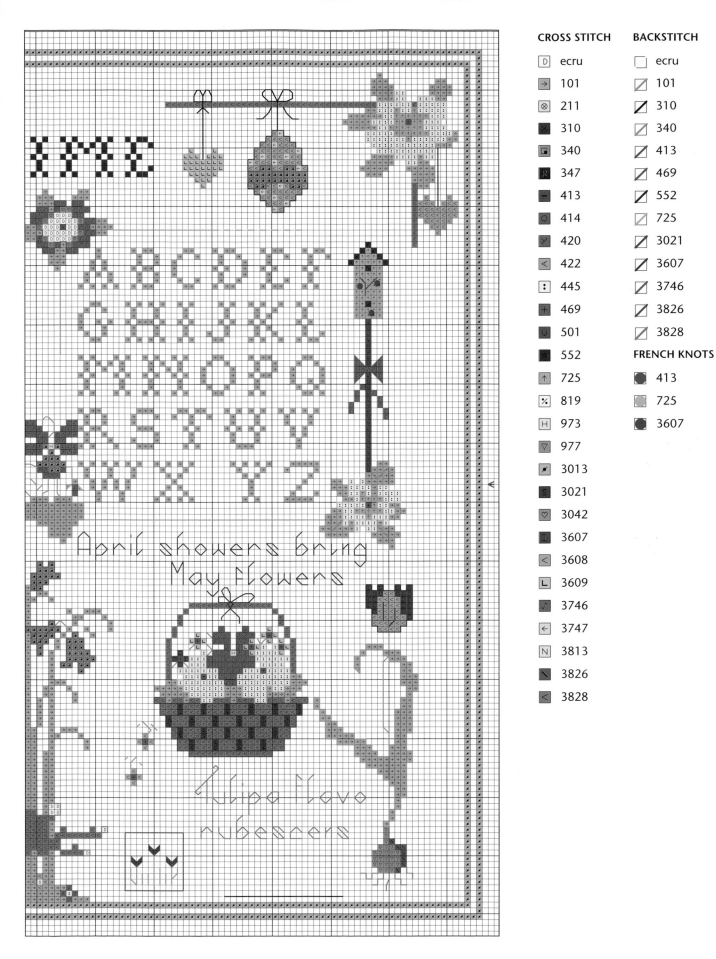

CROSS STITCH

D	ecru
→	101
⊗	211
✕	310
▣	340
R	347
–	413
O	414
Y	420
◁	422
:	445
+	469
U	501
▪	552
↑	725
%	819
H	973
▽	977
▪	3013
S	3021
♡	3042
▮	3607
◁	3608
L	3609
√	3746
←	3747
N	3813
◤	3826
◁	3828

BACKSTITCH

☐	ecru
◪	101
◪	310
◪	340
◪	413
◪	469
◪	552
◪	725
◪	3021
◪	3607
◪	3746
◪	3826
◪	3828

FRENCH KNOTS

●	413
●	725
●	3607

PASTORAL SAMPLER

This design was inspired directly by historical sources. I wanted to produce a small sampler with naïve animals set in the pastoral scenery so beloved of seventeenth century embroiderers, who were inspired by popular stumpwork embroideries. I found charming pictures of tapestry furnishings which showed fields, streams, running deer and spotted animals which I incorporated into this design to create a sampler with a bright, modern feel despite its historic roots.

| Finished size: 6 x 7½in (15 x 19cm) |
| Stitch count: 104 x 85 |

◆ 12 x 16in (30.5 x 41cm) 28 count linen in cream

◆ DMC stranded cottons as listed in the key

◆ Size 26 tapestry needle

1 Find the centre of the fabric and begin stitching here over two threads following the chart on page 23 using two strands of stranded cotton for the cross stitch and French knots and one for the stems in the border and the outlining. Use an embroidery frame if you wish.

2 When the stitching is complete press the sampler carefully and then frame (see Techniques page 125).

◆TIP◆

When using variegated thread you will get the best colour effects if you complete one whole cross stitch at a time rather than working in rows.

PASTORAL TRINKET POT

This useful little pot features one of the leaping deer from the Pastoral Sampler (see chart page 23).

◆ 3in (7.5cm) square of 28 count linen in cream

◆ Stranded cottons from the main key

◆ 3in (7.5cm) square of Vilene

◆ Wooden trinket pot (see Suppliers page 127)

1 Find the centre of the fabric and begin stitching here following the Pastoral Sampler chart using two strands of stranded cotton for the cross stitch.

2 When the stitching is complete, press the work and then iron the Vilene onto the back of the embroidery following the manufacturer's instructions.

3 Cut the embroidery to fit the trinket pot lid and assemble following the manufacturer's instructions.

The delightful Pastoral Sampler with its spin-off projects: a trinket pot and pincushion

SHEEP PINCUSHION

This useful little pincushion, which has its own chart, shows a charmingly rustic scene and features a novel black sheep button, available through Framecraft (see Suppliers page 127).

- ◆ **7in (18cm) square of 28 count linen in cream**
- ◆ **7in (18cm) square of cotton backing fabric**
- ◆ **DMC stranded cottons as listed in the key**
- ◆ **Polyester filling**
- ◆ **Mill Hill black sheep button**
- ◆ **16in (40cm) length of twisted cord made from matching threads**

1 Find the centre of the fabric and begin stitching here over two threads of linen following the chart below, using two strands of stranded cotton for the cross stitch and French knots.

2 When the stitching is complete, press the work and sew on the sheep button (if you are using one) with black sewing cotton.

3 Place the backing fabric and embroidery right sides together and stitch round three sides. Trim the seams, clip the corners, turn the right way out and stuff firmly. Sew up the fourth side.

4 Make a 16in (40cm) length of twisted cord from matching threads (see Techniques page 126) and slipstitch this all the way round the edge of the pincushion to finish off.

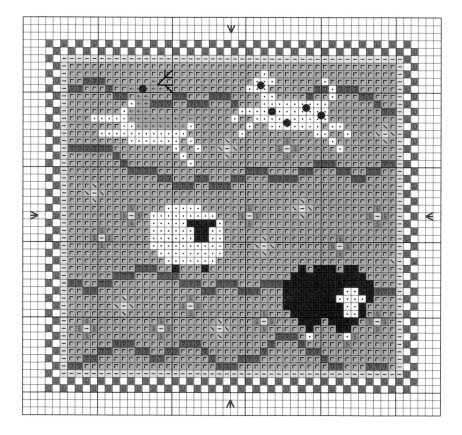

CROSS STITCH

·	blanc
Г	122 (variegated)
✗	310
S	340
=	470
↑	498
T	500
+	645
–	727
╲	778
U	798
○	3746
✕	3810
▽	3826
←	3827

BACKSTITCH

⊘	310
⊘	470
⊘	498

FRENCH KNOTS

●	310
●	3826

Note that the Sheep Pincushion shares the Pastoral Sampler key but only uses some of the threads

VALENTINE SAMPLER

This design is unashamedly romantic with its lace, hearts, roses and sentimental verse. Although I chose to stitch it as a Valentine it could be made for other romantic occasions, such as a wedding anniversary or simply to give to a loved one as a reminder of love's enduring qualities. This sampler inspired two spin-off designs – the Silver and Golden Wedding Samplers. They show how easy it is to adapt a design, to take certain key elements and give them a whole new slant by changing the colours used, choosing a different verse and highlighting various parts with beads or metallic threads. You could also look through the other charts in the book and substitute different motifs.

> **Finished size: 6 x 10in (15 x 25.5cm)**
> **Stitch count: 136 x 83**

- 12 x 20in (30.5 x 51cm) 28 count linen in lilac
- DMC stranded cottons as listed in the key
- Size 26 tapestry needle
- 6in (15cm) length of 1in (2.5cm) wide lace trimming in cream
- Mill Hill beads yellow (02002)
- Mill Hill beads rose (3045)
- Gold-coloured heart charm (optional)
- Beading needle

1 Find the centre of the fabric and begin stitching here over two threads of linen following the chart on page 29, using two strands of stranded cotton for the cross stitch and one strand for the backstitch. Use an embroidery frame if you wish.

2 When the embroidery is complete, slipstitch the length of lace to the linen one thread below the last line of stitching, using matching thread.

3 Add the beads to the flower centres and also dot some along the applied lace. Sew on the heart charm in the position indicated on the chart, or cross stitch a heart from the chart instead if you prefer.

4 Press the work carefully, avoiding the beads and charm if you have used them, and then frame (see Techniques page 125).

TIP

You could leave out the alphabet and use the space to personalise the sampler with a message or verse of your own to celebrate an anniversary or special occasion, see the box (right) and Designing and Planning a Sampler.

PERSONALISING YOUR SAMPLER

There are several alphabets on pages 119–121 which you could use to personalise your samplers and cards. Work out your names and dates on graph paper using pencils to start with for easy alteration. When you have worked out the details, count the number of squares from left to right and from the top of the tallest letter to the bottom square. Then centre the lines in the correct place on your design, checking and counting several times as you begin stitching. You could also look at other sources of lettering, such as calligraphy books, old samplers and special alphabet chart books.

SILVER WEDDING SAMPLER

Making samplers for special wedding anniversaries is one of the most popular pastimes for stitchers. This subtle and delicately coloured sampler (shown opposite) was adapted from the Valentine Sampler. If you wish to adapt this sampler for another anniversary, I have suggested a list of charms on page 28 that you could use. By changing the title and names using the alphabets provided on pages 119–121, and choosing colours to suit the anniversary, you could create your own special sampler.

> **Finished size: 5¾ x 9½in (14.5 x 24cm)**
> **Stitch count: 130 x 83**

- 10 x 18in (25.5 x 46cm) 28 count linen in beige
- DMC stranded cottons as listed in the key
- Caron Waterlilies thread, Fir
- 6in (15cm) length of white 1in (2.5cm) wide lace
- Mill Hill beads silver-lined (02010)
- Beading needle
- Silver-coloured heart charm

1 Find the centre of the fabric and begin stitching here over two threads of linen following the chart on page 30, using two strands of stranded cotton for the cross stitch and one strand for the backstitch. Use an embroidery frame if you wish.

2 When the embroidery is complete, slipstitch the length of lace to the linen three holes down from the last line of stitching, using white sewing cotton. Sew on the silver beads.

3 Sew on the heart charm with matching thread in the position indicated on the chart, or cross stitch a heart from the chart instead if you prefer. If you want to use a silver charm for this sampler but can only find gold ones, you can paint a gold charm with silver paint.

4 Press the work carefully, avoiding the beads and charm if you have used them, and then frame (see Techniques page 125).

GOLDEN WEDDING SAMPLER

Like the Silver Wedding Sampler, this design (shown opposite) is a variation on the Valentine Sampler. It is fascinating to see how changing one element – the colours – can so alter a design giving it a bolder look.

> **Finished size: 6 x 9½in (15 x 24cm)**
> **Stitch count: 128 x 83**

- 12 x 18in (30.5 x 46cm) 28 count linen in sand
- DMC stranded cottons as listed in the key
- DMC thread light gold 5282
- 6in (15cm) length of white lace approximately 1in (2.5cm) deep
- Mill Hill gold seed beads
- Beading needle
- Two gold-coloured heart charms and two gold bells

1 Find the centre of the fabric and begin stitching here over two threads of linen following the chart on page 31, using two strands of stranded cotton for the cross stitch and one strand for the backstitch. Use an embroidery frame if you wish.

2 Using one strand of gold thread, stitch whipped backstitch (see Stitch Library page 125) round the number section at the top of the sampler. Slipstitch the length of lace three holes down from the last row of stitching, using white thread.

3 Add the gold beads using pale orange thread and the beading needle. Add the gold charms (indicated by black dots) or stitch the heart motifs from the chart.

4 Press the work carefully, avoiding the beads and charms and frame (see Techniques page 125).

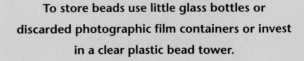

TIP

To store beads use little glass bottles or discarded photographic film containers or invest in a clear plastic bead tower.

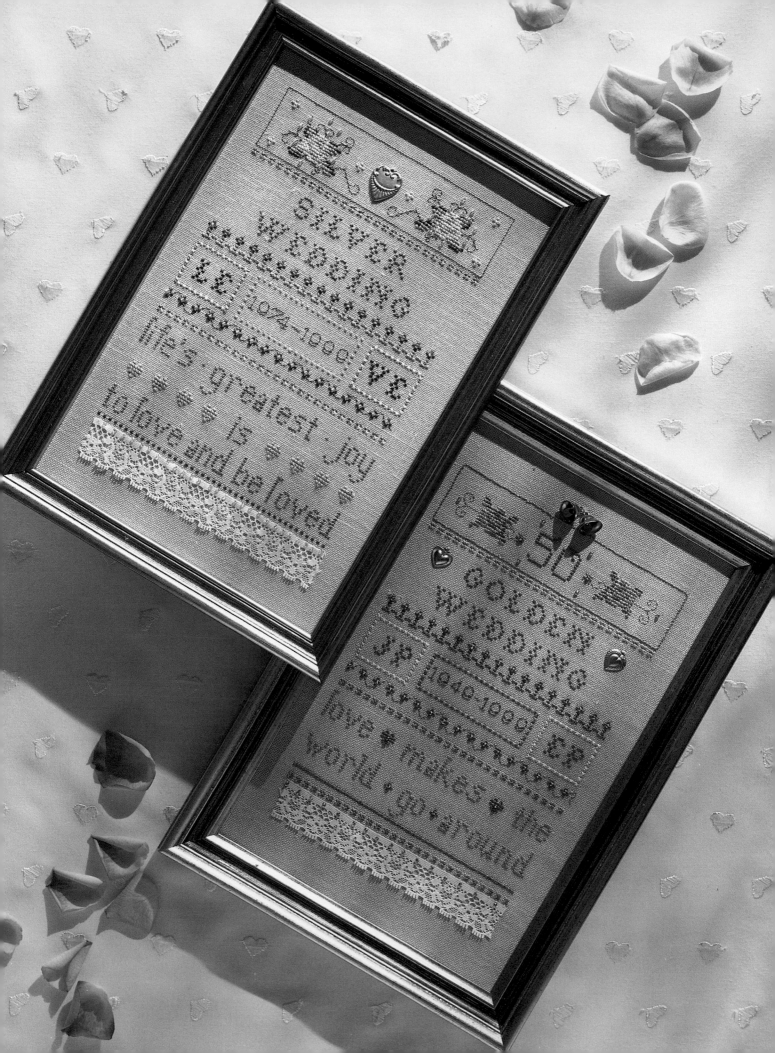

WEDDING ANNIVERSARIES

The following list suggests charms or embellishments suitable for the different anniversaries.

1st Paper

Tiny rolls of coloured paper with music or calligraphy, tied with ribbon and glued or stitched on.

2nd Cotton

Gold or silver cotton reel charms. Wind cotton round a tiny card bobbin.

3rd Leather

Tiny leather-covered buttons. Look in antique shops for delicate old ones in ivory shades.

4th Fruit

Ceramic buttons or silver or gold charms in the form of fruit (strawberries and apples are often the easiest to find).

5th Wood

Use some of the new-style wooden buttons in any shape which seems relevant to the recipients.

6th Sugar

Imitation sweet buttons, or miniature silver sugar tongs.

7th Wool

A sheep button, a cotton reel with fine wool wound onto it or a work basket button with knitting needles and balls of wool painted on.

8th Bronze

Paint any charm in a bronze finish, or use a coin.

9th Pottery

A teapot button, or a flower pot button.

10th Tin

A silver-coloured charm of any household item, like a bucket or kettle.

11th Steel

Cutlery charms.

12th Silk

Embroidery silk wound onto tiny cotton reel charms.

13th Lace

Buttons with lace effects painted on or a tiny piece of lace appliquéd with a heart charm with a lacy edge.

14th Ivory

Any charm which has an ivory colour would be suitable, or an elephant-shaped button.

15th Crystal

There are many charms made of crystal or resembling it and a heart would be a very suitable shape for a wedding anniversary.

20th China

A cup and saucer button or teapot button or charm.

25th Silver

Silver hearts, rings or any charm appropriate to the recipients.

30th Pearl

Pearl beads.

35th Coral

Beads in a coral colour or real coral beads from an antique shop.

40th Ruby

A ruby-coloured glass charm in the shape of a heart or flower.

45th Sapphire

A sapphire blue-coloured glass charm in a heart or flower shape.

50th Gold

Any gold charms, particularly hearts, rings, or something appropriate to the recipients.

55th Emerald

Green-coloured glass heart or flower.

60th Diamond

Any sparkly heart charm or a piece of diamanté jewellery.

CROSS STITCH

- 315
- 316
- 413
- 645
- 818
- 931
- 932
- 3041
- 3042
- 3046
- 3052
- 3752

BACKSTITCH

- 315
- 645

BEADS

- yellow
- rose

CROSS STITCH

⊙	blanc
↑	368
▽	501
U	754
⊙	819
—	3726

CROSS STITCH

CARON WATERLILIES

※	fir

BACKSTITCH

╱	501
╱	3726

BEADS

▢	silver

CROSS STITCH

- ⊙ ecru
- ▬ 223
- ▨ 471
- ▭ 977
- ▲ 3363
- ✕ 3776
- U 3827

BACKSTITCH

- ⧄ 977+5282 gold thread
- ⧄ 3776
- ⧄ 3363

BEADS

- ☐ gold

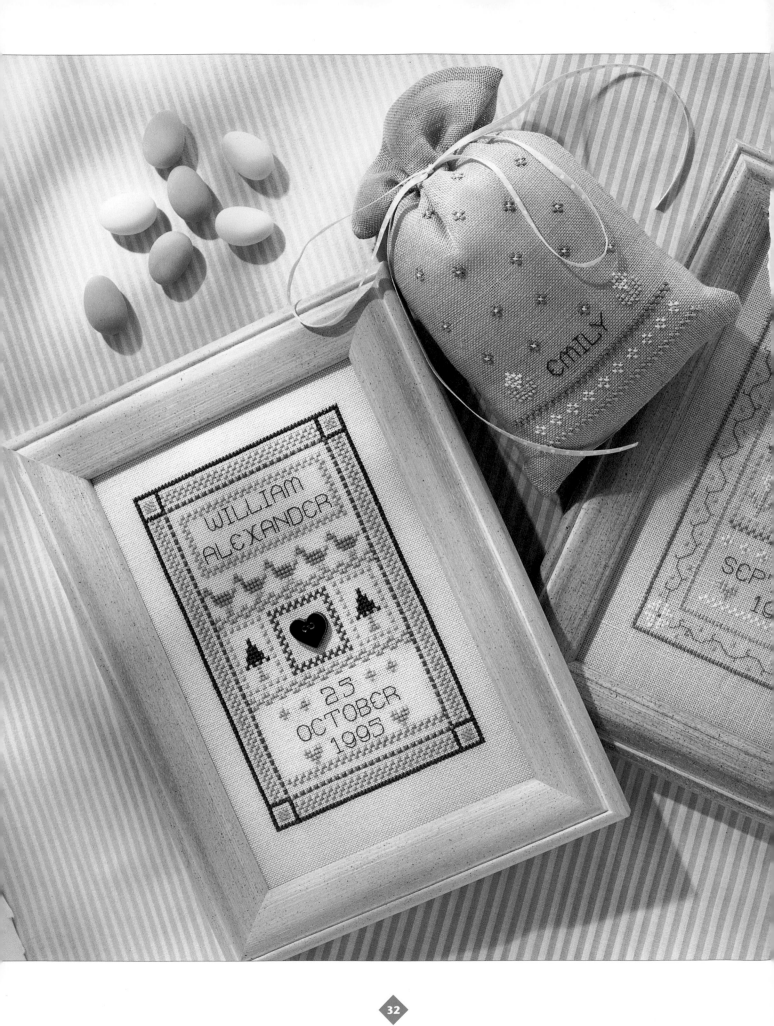

BIRTH SAMPLERS

Today we often stitch a sampler to celebrate a child's birth but this practice was not common in the past. It was more likely that a mourning sampler would be stitched on the loss of a family member. Most samplers were stitched by young girls and they often made genealogy samplers which included the names and birth dates of their parents and all the children in the family, so in a way these were the birth samplers of the time. Sometimes when a child died in infancy its name would be used again for a subsequent child. Sometimes the stitcher herself would die and the sampler would be finished by a sister or left unfinished. Now, thanks to improved health and social care, our smaller families and healthier babies mean each child can be celebrated, and what better way than to stitch them their very own sampler to keep always.

Shown here are two distinctive birth samplers for William and Sarah, designed so that they can be easily adapted for any child. Emily's Bag is a spin-off project which uses motifs and patterns from Sarah's Sampler

SARAH'S SAMPLER

This pretty design would be very suitable for a baby girl and could be stitched as a birth congratulations or as a christening sampler. The alphabet and numeral chart on page 119 will allow you to change the name and date. You could also substitute suitable motifs from the other charts in the book.

Finished size: 4¾ x 6¾in (12 x 17cm)
Stitch count: 96 x 66

- 8 x 12in (20 x 30.5cm) 28 count linen in pale pink
- DMC stranded cottons as listed in the key
- Size 26 tapestry needle
- Mill Hill tulip heart button (optional)

1 Find the centre of the fabric and begin stitching here over two threads of linen, following the chart on page 37 and using two strands of stranded cotton for the cross stitch and one for the backstitch. Use an embroidery frame if you wish.

2 When the stitching is complete, use matching thread to sew on the tulip heart button or stitch the heart from the chart in its place if you prefer.

3 Press the work carefully, avoiding the button, and then frame (see Techniques page 125).

WILLIAM'S SAMPLER

The layout of this design is similar to Sarah's Sampler but has a bolder look, created by the use of stronger colours. It is very easy and quick to stitch – ideal for a new arrival gift or a christening present.

Finished size: 4¾ x 6½in (12 x 16.5cm)
Stitch count: 91 x 60

- 8 x 12in (20 x 30.5cm) 30 count evenweave in pale blue
- DMC stranded cottons as listed in the key
- Size 26 tapestry needle
- Mill Hill denim heart button (optional)

1 Find the centre of the fabric and begin stitching here over two threads of linen following the chart on page 36, using two strands of stranded cotton for the cross stitch and one strand for the backstitch. Use an embroidery frame if you wish.

2 When the stitching is complete, sew on the heart button with blue thread, or stitch a heart motif from the chart instead.

3 Press the work carefully, avoiding the button, and then frame (see Techniques page 125).

ROSIE'S SAMPLER

This little version of William's Sampler (shown opposite) is stitched in bright colours as an alternative to the traditional boy and girl samplers. The border is omitted, which makes it even quicker to stitch. This sampler could be partly worked in advance of a baby's birth and the name and date added last in the space provided using the letters and numerals chart on page 119.

Finished size: 3½ x 5¾in (9 x 14.5cm)
Stitch count: 79 x 48

- 6 x 10in (15 x 25.5cm) 28 count evenweave in pale blue
- DMC stranded cottons as in the alternative key for William's Sampler
- Mill Hill red heart button (optional)

1 Follow the instructions for William's Sampler (left) but omit the border. Use the photograph on page 35 and the chart on page 36 but follow the alternative DMC colourway given.

2 When the stitching is complete, display the work, either framing as a picture or mounting in a greetings card (see Techniques page 126).

Delightful pieces from simple motifs: Rosie's Sampler, Sheep Hanging Sachets, Thomas Card and Small Gift Card

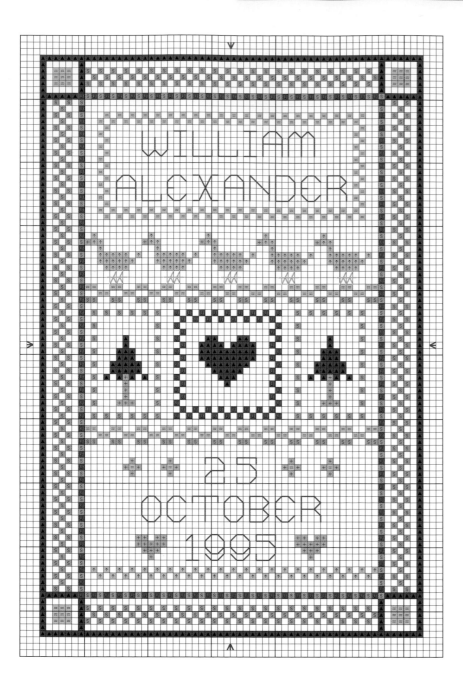

CROSS STITCH

↑ 318

U 333

= 341

+ 437

▲ 930

S 3042

BACKSTITCH

⟋ 437

⟋ 930

**ROSIE'S SAMPLER
ALTERNATE COLOURWAY**

- Use 3810 for duck's bodies, tree tops and outer border
- Use 472 for duck's beaks and feet, flower petals, border around trees and outer border
- Use 3607 for top border, tree trunks, border below trees, flower centres and hearts
- Use 798 for border below ducks and above flowers and all backstitch lettering
- Use 3746 for the central border and bottom border

THOMAS CARD

This little card (see page 35) uses motifs from William's Sampler, and can be quickly stitched as a gift which could be framed as a picture. You could substitute the motifs for others charted in the book.

◆ **5in (13cm) square of 28 count evenweave fabric in pale blue**

◆ **DMC stranded cottons from William's Sampler key**

◆ **5in (13cm) square of Vilene**

◆ **Blue card mount with 3¼ x 3½in (8.25 x 9cm) aperture**

1 Find the centre of the fabric and begin stitching over two threads, following William's Sampler chart and key above, using two strands of stranded cotton for the cross stitch and one for backstitch. Alter the name by using the alphabet chart on page 120.

2 When the stitching is complete, press the work and then iron a piece of Vilene onto the back of the embroidery, following the manufacturer's instructions.

3 Trim the design to fit the card and assemble (see Techniques on page 126).

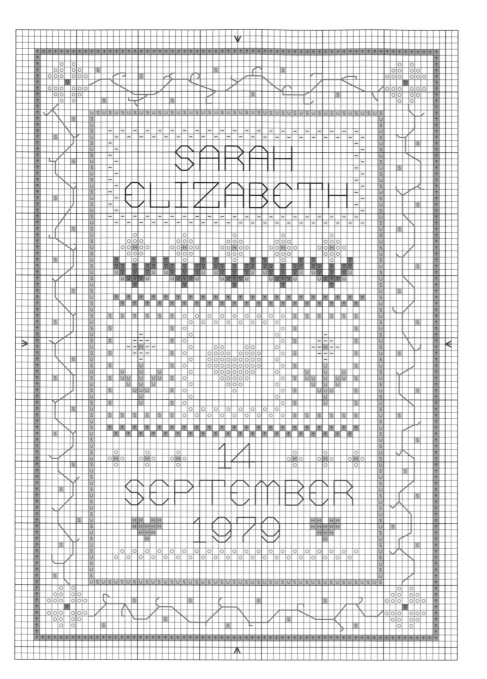

CROSS STITCH

○	ecru
↑	316
▽	502
∪	563
S	778
–	819
H	3827

BACKSTITCH

⧄	502
⧄	902
⧄	3726

SMALL GIFT CARD

Even the smallest card which has been hand stitched is very special and makes a keepsake of a unique occasion. This one (shown on page 35) uses the central heart and one of the flowers from Sarah's Sampler.

◆ 3 x 2in (7.5 x 5cm) 28 count linen in white
◆ DMC stranded cottons from Sarah's Sampler key
◆ 3 x 2in (7.5 x 5cm) piece of Vilene
◆ Card mount with 2½ x 1½in (6.25 x 3.75cm) aperture

1 Find the centre of the fabric and begin stitching here over two threads of linen following Sarah's Sampler chart and key above, using two strands of stranded cotton for the cross stitch.

2 When the design is complete, press and iron the Vilene onto the back according to the manufacturer's instructions.

3 Trim the design to fit the card and assemble (see Techniques on page 126).

SHEEP HANGING SACHETS

These pretty decorations, shown on page 35, which use motifs and borders from the Sarah and William Samplers, are designed to hang up in a nursery, perhaps packed with sweet-smelling herbs or pot-pourri.

For the blue sheep
◆ Two 5in (12.5cm) squares of 28 count evenweave fabric in pale blue
◆ DMC stranded cottons from William's Sampler key

For the pink sheep
◆ Two 5in (12.5cm) squares of 28 count linen in white
◆ DMC stranded cottons from Sarah's Sampler key

For each sheep
◆ Pale blue (or white) sewing cotton
◆ Small amount of polyester filling
◆ 12in (30cm) length of pale blue (or pink) decorative ribbon with a nursery design (see Suppliers page 127)
◆ Mill Hill white sheep button
◆ Dried lavender or pot-pourri (optional)

1 To stitch either the blue or pink sheep, find the centre of one of the linen squares and begin stitching here over two fabric threads. Use the photograph on page 35 as a guide to the design layout and stitch the chequered border and small flower motifs from the relevant main samplers charts (pages 36 and 37). Use two strands of stranded cotton and cross stitch.

2 When the stitching is complete, put the right sides together of both linen squares, securing the matching ribbon in the seam in the top left-hand corner, and sew round three sides of the sachet with matching sewing cotton. Trim the seams, clip the corners and turn right side out.

3 Sew on the sheep button with white sewing cotton, then stuff the sachet firmly, adding dried lavender or pot-pourri if desired. Finally, sew up the fourth side neatly.

EMILY'S BAG

This pretty gift bag, shown on page 32, could be given on the arrival of a new baby girl or contain a gift for a little girl's birthday. The name can be altered by using one of the alphabet charts provided on page 120.

Finished size: 5¼ x 8in (13.5 x 20cm) approximately

◆ Two 12 x 9in (30.5 x 23cm) pieces of 28 count linen in pink
◆ DMC stranded cottons from Sarah's Sampler key
◆ 15in (38cm) length of pale pink and white spotted narrow ribbon

1 Fold the first piece of linen in half vertically to find the middle, measure 3in (7.5cm) up from the bottom and find the centre stitch on the fold and begin work here. Use an embroidery frame if you wish.

2 Using the photograph of the bag on page 32 as a guide to the design layout, stitch the floral motifs and chequered lines from Sarah's Sampler chart page 37 over two threads of linen using two strands of stranded cotton for the cross stitch and one strand for the backstitch.

3 When the stitching is complete, measure 8½in (21.5cm) from the bottom and withdraw three threads. This is to thread the ribbon through later. Take the second piece of linen and make a ribbon row to match the first, then hem the top raw edges of both pieces.

4 With right sides together sew up both the long sides of the bag and along the bottom edge ¾in (2cm) from the bottom row of stitching. Trim the seams and clip the corners, then turn the bag the right way out.

5 Press the bag carefully and thread the pink and white spotted ribbon through the ribbon row and then tie in a bow.

APRIL SAMPLER

This sampler took its inspiration from the old verse about April, with its flowery spring theme. I decided to use forget-me-not blue to complement the colours of the primroses and daisies. The style and layout of the sampler is very much based on the traditional 'house and garden' kind which I like so much. Although the design is very traditional, the use of fresh, contemporary colours brings it up to date.

Finished size: 6½ x 9in (16.5 x 23cm)
Stitch count: 127 x 93

◆ **14 x 18in (36 x 46cm) 28 count linen in cream**
◆ **DMC stranded cottons as listed in the key**
◆ **Size 26 tapestry needle**

1 Find the centre of the fabric and using an embroidery frame if you wish begin stitching here following the chart on pages 42/43. Use two strands of stranded cotton over two threads of linen for the cross stitch, except for the following:
For the pathway use one strand and half cross stitch.
For the violet stems use two strands and backstitch.
For the butterfly wings use one strand for the outline and one strand and French knots (see Stitch Library page 124) for the dots on the wings.

2 When the stitching is complete, press the sampler carefully and frame (see Techniques page 125).

TIP

Stitch just the house to make a 'New Home' card, personalising it using the Lettering Library.

PRIMROSE POT BAND

This simple idea uses the primrose motif and chequered pattern from the April Sampler (see picture on page 40) and could be used to brighten up pots on the kitchen window-sill or turn a plant in a pot into a more personal gift for someone special.

◆ **18in (46cm) length of 1in (2.5cm) wide Aida band in white with mint green edge**
◆ **DMC stranded cottons from the main key**
◆ **Small piece of Velcro**

1 Fold the Aida band in half to find the centre and begin stitching here over one block using the April Sampler chart on pages 42/43 and referring to the photograph on page 40 as a guide to the design layout. Use two strands of stranded cotton for the cross stitch. Work outwards along the band, repeating the pattern as many times as necessary, first along one side and then the other.

2 When the embroidery is complete, fold under the ends of the band and stitch them down neatly with white sewing cotton. Press the work and then stitch small pieces of Velcro onto each end of the band to hold the band on the flowerpot.

STRAW HAT BAND

To make a pretty hat to shade you during gardening, this hearts and flowers band can be stitched very quickly using motifs from the main April Sampler. If you wish you could add a bunch of matching silk flowers.

◆ **22in (56cm) length of 1in (2.5cm) wide Aida band in white with pale blue edge**
◆ **DMC stranded cottons from the main key**
◆ **A straw hat**
◆ **Small bunch of silk flowers (optional)**

1 Fold the Aida band in half to find the centre and begin stitching here over one block. Follow the April Sampler chart on pages 42/43 and refer to the photograph below as a guide to the design layout. Use two strands of stranded cotton for the cross stitch, stitching one side of the band and then the other, repeating the pattern as many times as necessary.

2 When the stitching is complete, fold under the ends of the band and stitch down with white sewing cotton.

3 Press the work, then place the band on the hat and sew in position at the join with white sewing cotton, adding a bunch of silk flowers if you wish.

The fresh and cheerful April Sampler provided inspiration for a flower pot band (right) and a straw hat band (above)

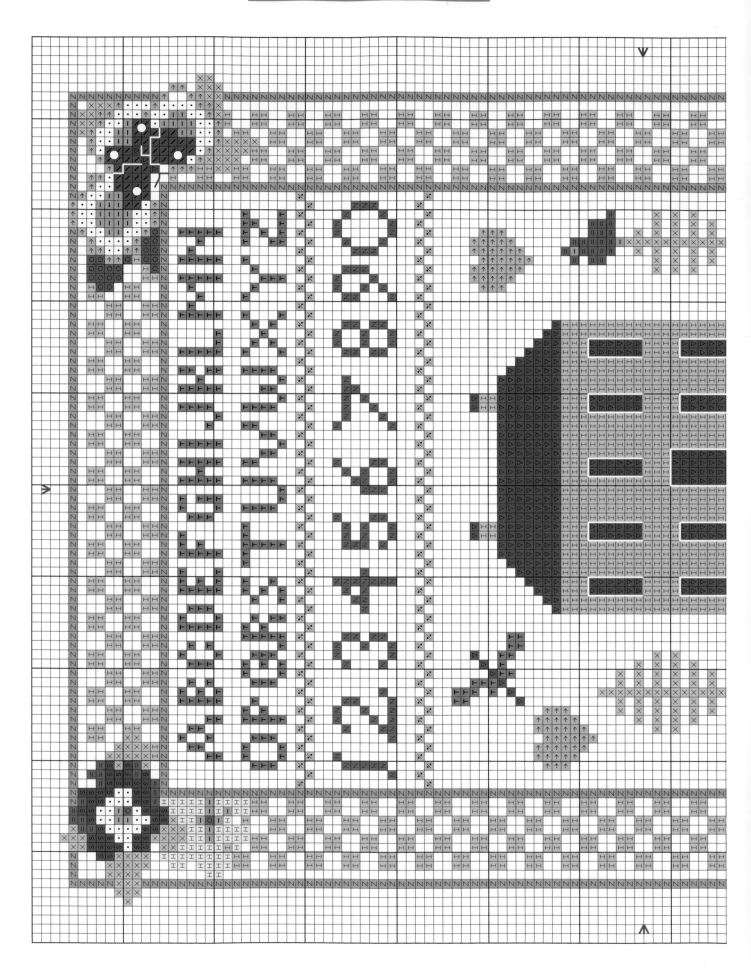

CROSS STITCH

·	blanc
X	125
S	315
N	340
H	341
◁	413

↑	3608
⊟	3726
T	3746
←	3776

◢	434
H	445
○	469
I	972
⊠	3013
N	3607

BACKSTITCH

◥	blanc
◳	125
◿	413
◹	3608

FRENCH KNOTS

○	blanc

In a

SUMMER

G

ABCDEFGH

Marig

IJKLMNO

PQRSTUV

What i

WXYZ

than

Flowers are nature's
jewels with whose
wealth she decks
her summer beauty

A swarm
of bees in
June is
worth a
silver
spoon

Foxglove

Gather herbs
and flowers for
posies + garlands

SUMMER GARDEN

This representation of a beautiful English country garden, with bright flowers, birds, butterflies and a fairy-tale cottage, is my second seasonal sampler based on traditional spot samplers. The shiny buttons echo the flower colours.

Finished size: 13½ x 10¼in (34 x 26cm)
Stitch count: 148 x 193

◆ 26 x 20in (66 x 51cm) 28 count evenweave in cream
◆ DMC stranded cottons as listed in the key
◆ Mill Hill seed beads in pale blue, black and crystal
◆ Mill Hill buttons (optional) – two pink bird-houses, one pansy, one bluebird
◆ Beading needle

1 Find the centre of the fabric and using an embroidery frame if you wish, begin stitching here over two threads of evenweave following the chart on page 48/49. Use two strands of stranded cotton for the cross stitch and one for the French knots, backstitch and outlining, except for the following: For the lettering use one strand except for the words 'Marigold Cottage' which use two strands. For the tendrils round the strawberries and the morning glory use two strands and backstitch. Use the Lettering Library to stitch your initials and date.

2 Sew the beads onto the dragonfly and spider's web with matching thread and the beading needle.

3 When the embroidery is complete, sew on the buttons with matching threads if you are using them or stitch the motifs from the chart instead.

4 Press the sampler, avoiding any beads or buttons, and frame (see Techniques page 125).

SUMMER GARDEN TABLECLOTH

This pretty flowery cloth will make afternoon tea in the garden really special, re-combining various motifs from the Summer Garden Sampler in a charmingly fresh design (see chart on pages 48/49).

◆ 32 x 36in (81 x 92cm) 28 count evenweave fabric in white

◆ DMC stranded cottons from the main key

◆ 4yd (4m) of white lace edging

1 Find the centre of the fabric and begin stitching here over two fabric threads using two strands of stranded cotton for the cross stitch and one for the backstitch. Use an embroidery frame if you wish. Refer to the photograph below for the design layout. Start in the centre with the rose motif from the Summer Garden Sampler, adding bees at random.

2 To work out where to place the four 'corner' motifs, adjoining 'dotted' lines and lettering, measure

out from the central starting point. Stitch the 'dotted' lines and corner motifs about 4⅛in (10.5cm) out from the centre. Add the lettering beneath the lines, about 3½in (9cm) out from the centre point. Follow the quotation on the main Spring Time Sampler (page 48/49) beginning, 'Flowers are nature's'. Use graph paper if you wish to chart out all these elements before you stitch.

3 When the central panel is complete, stitch the remainder of the flower, fruit and insect motifs randomly over the cloth, choosing the motifs from the main chart. You can do this by eye or by placing pins at regular intervals across the cloth to mark their places. Turn the cloth so the motifs are scattered and not all the same way up.

4 When the stitching is complete, turn a small hem round the edge and sew on the lace with white sewing cotton. Press carefully to finish.

TIP

As table linen requires frequent washing make sure you use a reputable, colourfast brand of thread, like DMC or Anchor. See page 125 for washing and ironing instructions.

STRAWBERRY NAPKIN

This features the strawberry motif from the central area of the Summer Garden Sampler chart (pages 48/49). It is quick to stitch so you could make a set to accompany strawberry teas. Stitch on a white lace-edged napkin for embroidery approximately 15in (38cm) square, using DMC stranded cottons from the main key and two strands for the cross stitch. Mark the positions of the strawberries at regular intervals with pins, turning the napkin around to vary them.

The pretty spin-off projects from the main Summer Garden Sampler: tablecloth, strawberry napkin and napkin ring, decorative teaspoon, jar lacy and gift card

STRAWBERRY NAPKIN RING

To hold the napkin why not make a napkin holder? Use the strawberry design from the central area of the Summer Garden Sampler chart. Stitch on a 2 x 1½in (5 x 4cm) piece of 14 count Aida (or to fit into your napkin holder), using DMC stranded cottons from the main key. Use two strands for the cross stitch and one strand for the backstitch stems and outer border. When complete, press and slot into a Perspex napkin holder (see Suppliers page 127).

SILVER TEASPOON

To make tea-time special, add this decorative teaspoon which uses the strawberry motif from the central area of the Summer Garden sampler (chart pages 48/49). You will need a silver teaspoon for embroidery (see Suppliers page 127). Stitch the strawberry, using two strands of DMC stranded cotton for the cross stitch, in the centre of the piece of Aida provided with the spoon handle. When complete, insert into the handle.

STRAWBERRY JAR LACY

Continuing the fruit theme this jar lacy would add a special touch to any jar of strawberry jam, especially a home-made gift. Stitch the strawberry motif from the central area of the Summer Garden Sampler chart (pages 48/49) in the centre of a white jar lacy for embroidery, using two strands of DMC stranded cotton for the cross stitch and one strand for the backstitch. Add bees around the fruit and spot cross stitches in light green (471) randomly over the lacy. Insert a ½yd (0.5m) length of narrow red ribbon to complete.

STRAWBERRY GIFT CARD

This uses the strawberry and bee motif from the central area of the Summer Garden Sampler and could accompany any home-made gift. Stitch the strawberry in the centre of a 2in (5cm) square of 28 count sand-coloured linen, over two fabric threads using two strands of DMC stranded cotton for the cross stitch. Iron a piece of Vilene onto the back of the embroidery then mount into a 2in (5cm) square card mount with a circular aperture (see Techniques page 125).

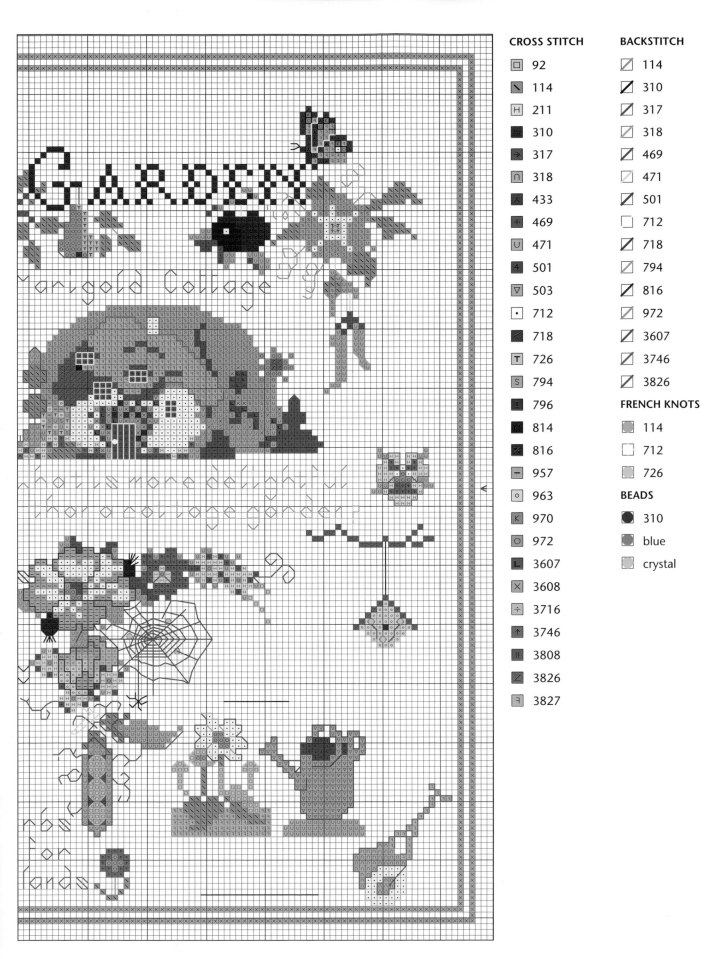

CROSS STITCH		BACKSTITCH	
□	92	◿	114
◥	114	◿	310
H	211	◿	317
▦	310	◿	318
→	317	◿	469
∩	318	◿	471
⅄	433	◿	501
+	469	☐	712
U	471	◿	718
◢	501	◿	794
▽	503	◿	816
·	712	◿	972
<	718	◿	3607
T	726	◿	3746
S	794	◿	3826
⊥	796	**FRENCH KNOTS**	
▨	814	▨	114
◪	816	☐	712
−	957	▨	726
○	963	**BEADS**	
K	970	●	310
O	972	●	blue
▤	3607	▨	crystal
✕	3608		
÷	3716		
↑	3746		
‖	3808		
▨	3826		
⊒	3827		

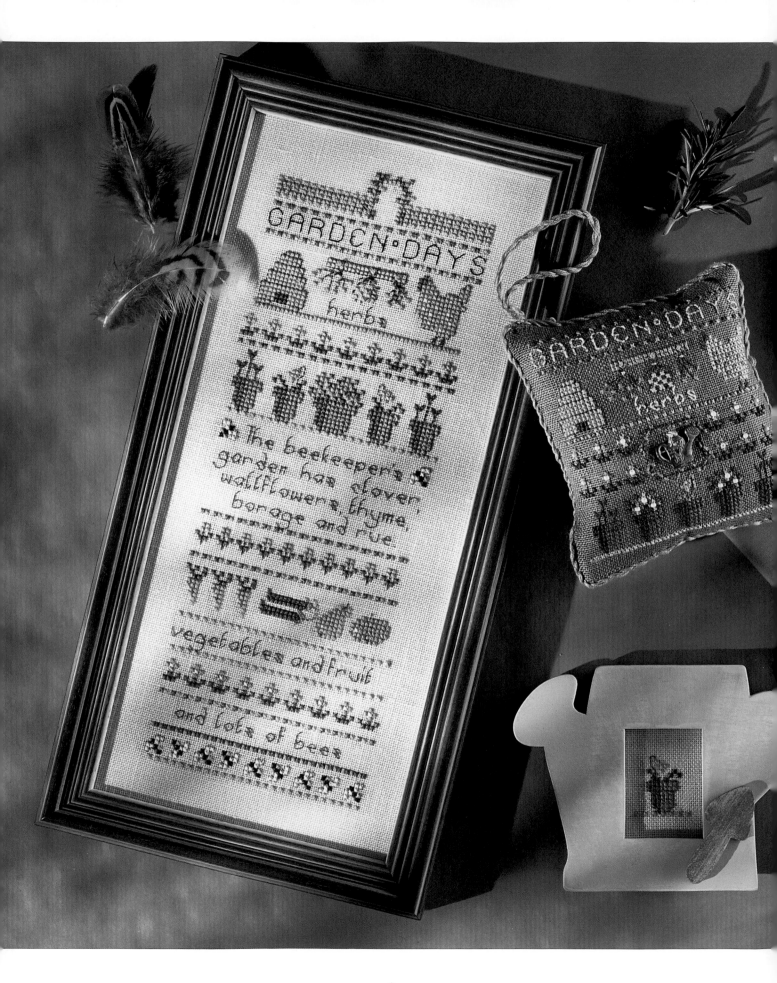

GARDEN DAYS SAMPLER

Designed along the lines of a traditional band sampler, this sampler was inspired by old-fashioned cottage gardens, where bees and hens were kept and where vegetables, herbs and fruit grew among flowers. The band-type layout makes the design highly flexible, allowing you to adapt the overall look and use individual elements as smaller projects.

Finished size: 10½ x 3¾in (27 x 9.5cm)
Stitch count: 143 x 52

◆ **20 x 9in (51 x 23cm) 28 count linen in cream**
◆ **DMC stranded cottons as listed in the key**
◆ **Size 26 tapestry needle**

1 Find the centre of the fabric and begin stitching over two threads following the chart on page 53, using two strands of stranded cotton for the cross stitch and one for lettering, outlining and all stems. For the hanging herbs pegs use French knots with two strands.

2 When the stitching is complete, press the sampler carefully and then frame (see Techniques page 125).

GARDEN DAYS BOOKMARK

This bookmark is stitched on a 2 x 7in (5 x 17cm) piece of 28 count linen in summer khaki. Chose two of the flowers in pots from the Garden Days Sampler chart, page 53 and stitch evenly and alternately down the bookmark over two fabric threads, using two strands of stranded cotton for the cross stitch and one for the backstitch and outlining. When complete, iron Vilene onto the back. Trim and mount into a ready-made bookmark (see Suppliers page 127).

The Garden Days Sampler with its spin-off projects:

a bookmark, pincushion and two pictures

GARDEN DAYS PINCUSHION

This pincushion design (see page 50) is a contemporary one but with a traditional feel. It has its own chart and uses a more unusual, darker shade of linen combined with light threads for an interesting and modern effect.

- Two 8in (20cm) squares of 28 count linen in grey blue
- DMC stranded cottons as in the key
- Watering-can charm (optional, from Framecraft)
- Mill Hill white seed beads
- Beading needle
- 26in (66cm) length of hand-made twisted cord in purple and pink
- Small amount of polyester filling

1 Find the centre of one of the pieces of linen and begin stitching here over two threads following the chart below, using two strands of stranded cotton for the cross stitch, French knots and the backstitch and one strand for the outlining. Use a flexihoop if you wish.

2 When the embroidery is complete, sew on the watering-can charm (or replace with a stitched motif from the chart) and add the beads with the beading needle. Press the work carefully, avoiding the beads and charm.

3 To make up into a pincushion, take the second piece of linen and place right sides together with the embroidered piece and stitch around three sides. Trim off the excess fabric all round, clip the corners, turn right side out and stuff the pincushion firmly with some polyester filling. Use tiny stitches to close the fourth side.

4 Make a twisted cord from purple and pink stranded cotton about 26in (66cm) long (see Techniques page 126). Using toning sewing cotton, stitch the cord round the outer edge, forming a loop at the top left-hand corner so that the pincushion can be hung up if wished.

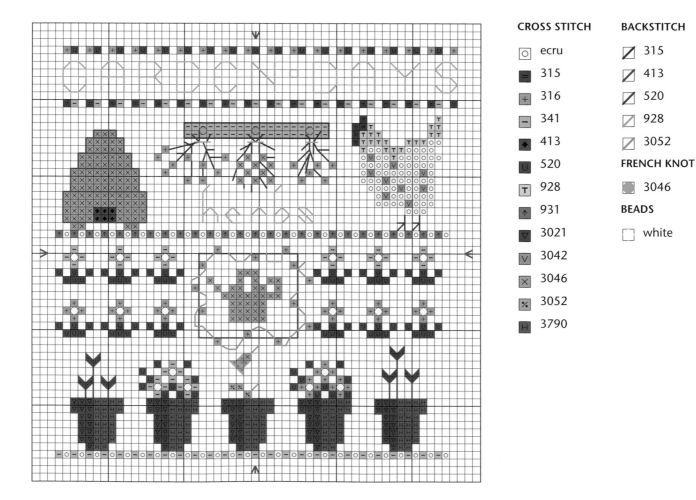

CROSS STITCH		BACKSTITCH	
⊙	ecru	╱	315
▬	315	╱	413
+	316	╱	520
–	341	╱	928
◆	413	╱	3052
U	520	**FRENCH KNOT**	
T	928	▨	3046
↑	931	**BEADS**	
▼	3021	☐	white
V	3042		
X	3046		
%	3052		
H	3790		

GARDEN DAYS PICTURES

These little pictures (shown on page 50) use simple motifs from the main Garden Days Sampler and make ideal gifts. The garden theme frames add much to their appeal and it is worth looking for unusual frames for possible stitching projects (see Suppliers page 127). Stitch each picture on a 3in (8cm) square of 28 count cream linen. Chose a flower in a pot from the row near the top of the Garden Days Sampler chart (right) and work from the centre of the fabric over two threads, using two strands of DMC stranded cotton for the cross stitch and one for the backstitch and outlining. Press the work and iron a piece of Vilene onto the back, then trim the embroidery to fit the frame.

CROSS STITCH

○	ecru
■	310
☰	315
+	316
◆	413
✕	422
K	501
◨	729
−	794
▽	840
H	841
✕	3051

BACKSTITCH

◿	310
◿	315
◿	413
◿	501
◿	729
◿	840
◿	3051

FRENCH KNOT

▦	329

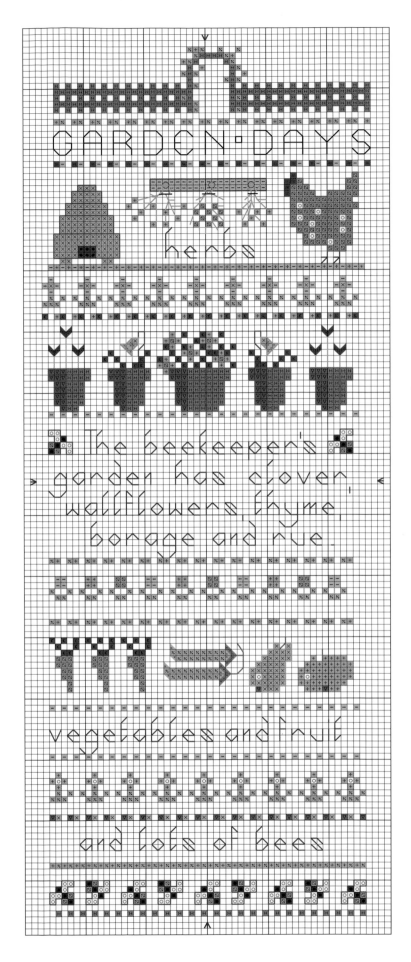

GATHER THE FLOWERS SAMPLER

This small sampler is one of my more contemporary ones in its style and layout. I wanted to use the lovely shiny mauve pansy buttons and thought they looked very pretty against the subtle Belfast linen. I stitched the quotation and decided to continue the garden theme it evoked by including the little watering-can. If you prefer not to use the pansy buttons, a mauve pansy is charted for you to stitch instead. This design would also look good made up as a pincushion.

Finished size: 4¼ x 4in (11 x 10cm)
Stitch count: 59 x 57

◆ 8in (20cm) square of 32 count Belfast linen in raw linen
◆ DMC stranded cottons as listed in the key
◆ Size 26 tapestry needle
◆ Two pansy buttons (optional)

1 Find the centre of the fabric and begin stitching here over two threads of linen following the chart

below, using two strands of stranded cotton for the cross stitch, two strands for the backstitch lettering and one strand for the outlining. Use a hoop to keep the work taut if you wish.

2 When the embroidery is complete, sew on the pansy buttons with matching thread or stitch the pansy motif from the chart instead.

3 Press the work carefully, avoiding the buttons if used, and frame (see Techniques page 125).

CROSS STITCH

D	ecru
■	310
L	369
◥	437
▽	502
N	726
■	814
–	3609
✓	3746
U	3768

BACKSTITCH

⁄	310
⁄	433
⁄	502
⁄	3746
⁄	3768

SEASHELL COTTAGE SAMPLER

Cornish holidays and living mainly on the north-west coast of England, have contributed to this design. The cottage was inspired by the fishermen's cottages of Cornwall, with their higgledy-piggledy appearance, clustered around the harbour. I love the many-changing blues and aquas of seaside light and its intensity, and of course the sight (and sound) of seagulls never far away.

Finished size: 8 x 6½in (20 x 16.5cm)
Stitch count: 112 x 90

◆ **16 x 13in (40 x 33cm) 28 count linen in white**
◆ **DMC stranded cottons as listed in the key**
◆ **Size 26 tapestry needle**
◆ **Beading needle**
◆ **White sewing cotton**
◆ **Two gold-coloured seashell charms**
  (optional – see Suppliers page 127)
◆ **Mill Hill frosted blue beads (62043)**

1 Find the centre of the fabric and begin stitching here over two threads of linen following the chart on page 58 and working outwards. Use an embroidery frame to keep your work taut if you wish. Use two strands of stranded cotton for the cross stitch and one for the French knots, except for the following:
For the sea use one strand and cross stitch.
For the sky use one strand and half cross stitch.
For the seaweed use one strand and cross stitch.
For the bucket handle use one strand and whipped backstitch (see Stitch Library page 125).
For the backstitch use one strand, except for the side of the door (in dark grey) which uses two strands.

2 When the stitching is complete, sew on the seashell charms and blue beads, using the white sewing cotton and the beading needle.

3 Press carefully, avoiding the beads and charms, then frame (see Techniques page 125).

TIP

When sewing on the beads use a whole cross stitch rather than the normally suggested half cross stitch as this will make the bead more secure.

CROSS STITCH

·	blanc	↑	437	▲	930
L	356	S	469	✕	958
+	413	−	518	○	964
U	415	▽	519	◿	3727
⊠	436	=	739		

HALF CROSS STITCH

◿	519

BACKSTITCH

◿	356	◿	518
◿	413	◿	930
◿	415	◿	958
◿	436		
◿	469		

FRENCH KNOTS

●	413
□	415
●	930

BEADS

●	frosted blue

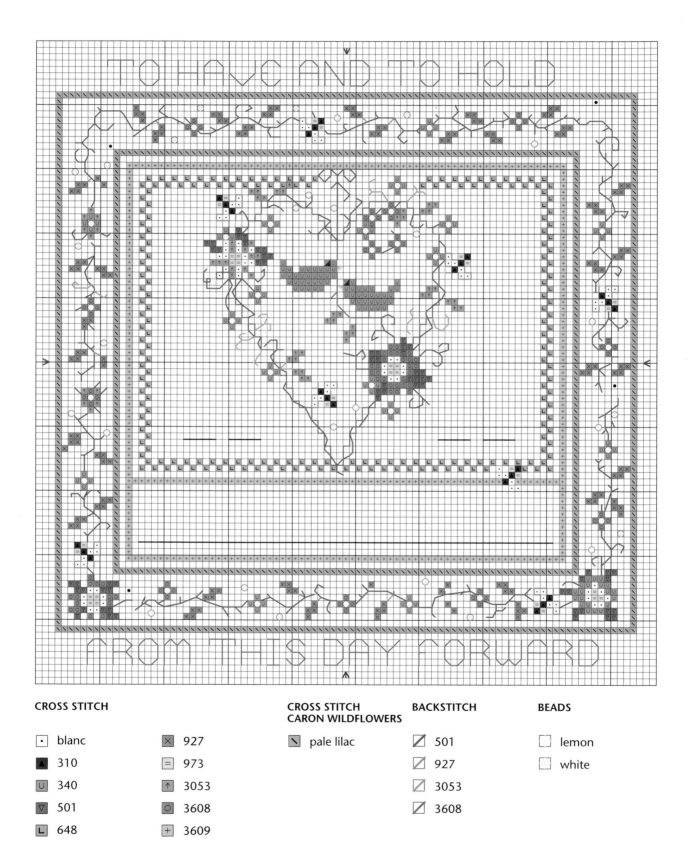

CROSS STITCH

·	blanc	✕	927
▲	310	=	973
U	340	↑	3053
▽	501	O	3608
L	648	+	3609

CROSS STITCH CARON WILDFLOWERS

◣	pale lilac

BACKSTITCH

◿	501
◿	927
◿	3053
◿	3608

BEADS

☐	lemon
☐	white

To Have and to Hold Wedding Sampler

One of the most enjoyable aspects of designing samplers is the variety of effects we can create, especially using the interesting threads, beads and embellishments that are available today. This design (shown on page 63) was intended to be really pretty and to celebrate the most romantic of days in soft shades, and with delicate additions like pearl beads and tiny gold charms. The sampler would make a very special gift and if you don't wish to stitch the whole sampler there are many smaller items you can make instead.

Finished size: 6½ x 7in (16.5 x 18cm)
Stitch count: 94 x 91

- 12in (30.5cm) square of 28 count linen in antique white
- DMC stranded cottons as listed in the key
- Caron Wildflowers thread, Pale Lilac
- Size 26 tapestry needle
- Beading needle
- Mill Hill seed beads in lemon and white
- Gold charms (optional, from Framecraft) – butterfly, flower basket, flower and heart

1 Find the centre of the fabric and begin stitching here over two threads of linen, following the chart on page 59 and using an embroidery frame if you wish. Use two strands of stranded cotton for the cross stitch except for the following:
For all the cross stitch with the Wildflowers thread use only one strand.

For the inner pink border use one strand and cross stitch.
For the outlining and backstitch use one strand.

2 To stitch the initials and date, use the alphabet and numerals charted on pages 119 and 120, positioning them on the black lines shown on the chart (use graph paper to achieve the correct spacing). Use DMC 340 to cross stitch the initials and DMC 648 for the date.

3 When the stitching is complete, sew on the seed beads using matching sewing thread and the beading needle, and then sew on the various charms if you are using them. The black dots on the chart indicate their positions.

4 Press the sampler carefully, avoiding all the beads and charms used, and then frame (see Techniques page 125).

WEDDING SACHET

This sachet (see page 62) uses motifs and patterns from the To Have and To Hold Wedding Sampler – what prettier way to present a gift to the bride and groom? It could also hold sugared almonds or pot-pourri.

◆ **Two pieces 6 x 9½in (15 x 24cm) 28 count linen in white**

◆ **Stranded cottons from the main key**

◆ **Seed beads in white and yellow**

◆ **Beading needle**

◆ **5in (13cm) piece of white lace**

◆ **Gold heart charm**

◆ **5in (13cm) length of ¼in white satin ribbon**

1 Start working the floral band approximately 1in (2.5cm) from the bottom of one of the pieces of linen following the main chart on page 59 and using the photograph on page 62 as a guide to the design layout. Use two strands of stranded cotton for the cross stitch and one strand for the backstitch and Caron thread. Stitch your own initials and date using the alphabet and numerals charted on pages 119 and 120.

2 When the embroidery is complete, add the lace by slipstitching it in the position indicated by the photograph. Sew on the beads with matching thread and the beading needle, and then add the heart charm if you are using it.

3 Measure 2½in (6.5cm) up from the top row of stitching and carefully withdraw three threads. Using the antique hemming method (see Stitch Library page 123), make a hem using one strand of white stranded cotton. Measure 1¼in (3cm) from the hem row and withdraw three threads to form the row to thread the ribbon through.

4 Take the second piece of linen, which will form the plain back of the gift bag, and measuring carefully withdraw three threads for the ribbon row and three threads for the hem and complete to match the front of the bag.

5 With right sides together sew up the side seams and along the bottom of the two pieces of linen. Press the seams and clip the corners to reduce bulk. Turn the bag the right way out and thread the white satin ribbon through the withdrawn row, pull up and tie.

GIFT CARD

This little card (shown on page 63) uses motifs from the main To Have and To Hold Sampler and could be stitched to accompany one of the other gifts in a co-ordinating set. On a 2 x 3in (5 x 7.5cm) piece of white 28 count linen stitch the birds and a few small random flower motifs from the main chart on page 59, over two threads of linen using two strands of stranded cotton for the cross stitch and one for the backstitch. Stitch yellow seed beads to the centres of the flowers. When complete, iron a piece of Vilene onto the back. Trim to fit a white card mount with a 2¼in (5.75cm) oval aperture and assemble (see Techniques page 126).

TRINKET POT

This trinket pot (shown below), uses a flower motif from the To Have and To Hold Sampler and would make an attractive bridesmaids' present. Find the centre of a 3in (7.5cm) square of white 28 count linen and begin stitching here over two fabric threads following the main chart on page 59, using two strands of stranded cotton for the cross stitch and one strand for the backstitch. When complete, iron a piece of Vilene onto the back. Mount in a trinket pot (see Suppliers page 127) according to the manufacturer's instructions.

RING PILLOW

This pretty cushion (shown opposite) will keep wedding rings secure before the ceremony and will be treasured as a special souvenir afterwards. It uses motifs from the To Have and To Hold Wedding Sampler.

Finished size: 5¼in (13.5cm) square approximately

- ◆ Two 8in (20.5cm) squares of 28 count linen in white
- ◆ Stranded cottons from the main key
- ◆ Seed beads in white and yellow
- ◆ Beading needle
- ◆ Small gold heart charm
- ◆ 25in (63cm) length of white lace for edging
- ◆ 12in (30.5cm) length narrow ribbon in pale pink polka dot
- ◆ Polyester filling

1 Find the centre of one of the pieces of linen and begin stitching here following the main chart on page 59, using the photograph (right) as a guide to the design layout. Use two strands of stranded cotton for the cross stitch and one strand for the backstitch and Caron thread. Stitch the lettering and names from the alphabet charted on pages 119 and 120.

2 When the embroidery is complete, sew on the beads with matching thread and the beading needle and then add the heart charm.

3 Cut the ribbon in half and using sewing cotton stitch a matching piece on either side of the central flower motif. The wedding rings can be tied to these.

4 Taking the second piece of linen, match it right sides together with the embroidered piece. Trim the edges and insert the lace into the seam, then sew round three sides. Turn the cushion the right way out and stuff firmly, then sew up the fourth side, catching the lace neatly in the seam as you do so.

The lovely To Have and To Hold Sampler with trinket pot, wedding sachet, ring pillow and gift card

ELIZABETHAN GARDEN SAMPLER

This sampler contains many traditional band patterns, some of which date back to the seventeenth century. The design is a modern interpretation and is quite formal and structured. The poem describes the delights of Elizabethan gardens and is interspersed with patterns as some of the earliest band samplers would have been. These band designs – the gillyflowers (carnations), key pattern, strawberries and bees – are very versatile and could decorate all kinds of items.

> **Finished size: 14½ x 5in (37 x 12.5cm)**
> **Stitch count: 207 x 72**

- ◆ **28 x 15in (71 x 38cm) 28 count linen in antique white**
- ◆ **DMC stranded cottons as listed in the key**
- ◆ **Caron Wildflowers thread, Painted Desert and Pale Lilac**
- ◆ **Caron Waterlilies thread, Spruce**
- ◆ **Size 26 tapestry needle**

1 Find the centre of the fabric and begin stitching here over two threads of linen, following the chart on pages 68/69 and using an embroidery frame if you wish. Use one strand of stranded cotton for the cross stitch except for the following:
For the gillyflowers use two strands.
For the white pattern in the bee border and the bee bodies use two strands.
For the small tulip border use two strands of pale pink (3727).

For the heartsease and the white cross stitch in that border use two strands.

2 Complete the stitching and then personalise the sampler by stitching the initials and date of your choice, using the alphabet and numbers charted on pages 119 and 120.

3 Finally, press the sampler carefully and frame (see Techniques on page 125).

> **TIP**
>
> Try not to carry your thread across the back of your work for more than a couple of stitches, especially on a light coloured linen as it will show through as dark lines on the front and spoil the work.

GREEK KEY HAND TOWEL

This design has been seen in many forms from ancient times. It is simple to stitch and always looks sophisticated and classical. You will need a white cotton hand towel approximately 12 x 20in (30.5 x 51cm) and a 14in (35.5cm) length of 1in (2.5cm) wide Aida band in white with a mint green edge. Start stitching from the centre of the band, three holes up from the bottom, following the key pattern from the Elizabethan Garden Sampler chart on pages 68/69 and work the cross stitch over one block using one strand of stranded cotton throughout. Work until the band fits your towel width. Press and turn the ends in, pinning the band on the towel and slipstitching into place with matching sewing cotton.

STRAWBERRIES TEA TOWEL

Stitching the strawberry border from the Elizabethan Garden Sampler would turn a tea towel gift into something special. You will need a pink-and-white check cotton tea towel and a 22in (56cm) length of 2in (5cm) wide Aida band in white with a white edge. Start stitching from the centre of the band over one block, three holes up from the bottom, following the Elizabethan Garden Sampler chart on pages 68/69 and using one strand of stranded cotton. Add a single line of cross stitch above and below the strawberries using one strand of Caron Wildflowers thread Painted Desert. Work until the band fits your tea towel width. Press and turn the ends in, pinning the band on the towel and slipstitching into place with matching sewing cotton.

BEES TEA TOWEL

This border has a contemporary look although bees have appeared in textiles from early times. Bees represent industry and so are appropriate on such a useful household textile. You will need a beige-and-white check cotton tea towel and a 20in (51cm) length of 2in (5cm) wide Aida band in white with white edge. Start stitching from the centre of the band, four holes up from the bottom, following the Elizabethan Garden Sampler chart on pages 68/69 and

using two strands of stranded cotton for the bee bodies and one strand for the outlining and green cross stitch. Omit the white cross stitch. Add a border line of alternate cross stitches above and below the bees using mink brown (840). Work until the band fits your tea towel width. Press and turn the ends in, pinning the band on the towel and slipstitching into place with matching sewing cotton.

GILLYFLOWER HAND TOWEL

The many attractive patterned bands of the Elizabethan Garden Sampler (see photograph on page 65) lend themselves to decorate towel and tea towel bands very well. The carnations, or gillyflowers as the Elizabethans called them, are a great favourite with designers and have been for centuries and this particular band shows a Persian influence in its design.

◆ **White cotton hand towel approximately 12 x 20in (30.5 x 51cm)**

◆ **14in (35.5cm) length of 2in (5cm) wide Aida band in white with white edge**

◆ **Stranded cottons from the main key**

1 Find the centre of the Aida band and begin stitching here over one block, six holes up from the bottom of the band and following the Elizabethan Sampler chart on pages 68/69. Work in cross stitch, using two strands of stranded cotton for the gillyflowers and one strand for the lines of cross stitch which form a border along the top and bottom of the flowers. Work outwards along the band, first one side and then the other until the band fits your towel width.

2 Press the work and turn the ends in, pinning the band in position on the towel and slipstitching into place with matching sewing cotton, and finally pressing again.

The useful spin-off projects based on the Elizabethan Garden Sampler: the Greek key hand towel, strawberries tea towel, bees tea towel and gillyflower hand towel

CROSS STITCH

- ○ blanc
- ∪ 340
- ‖ 422
- ✕ 500
- ← 840
- ∣ 3727

CROSS STITCH CARON WILDFLOWERS

- s pale lilac
- ◼ painted desert

CROSS STITCH CARON WATERLILIES

- ◁ spruce

BACKSTITCH

- ◹ 340
- ◹ 422
- ◹ 500
- ◹ 840

BACKSTITCH CARON WILDFLOWERS

- ◹ painted desert

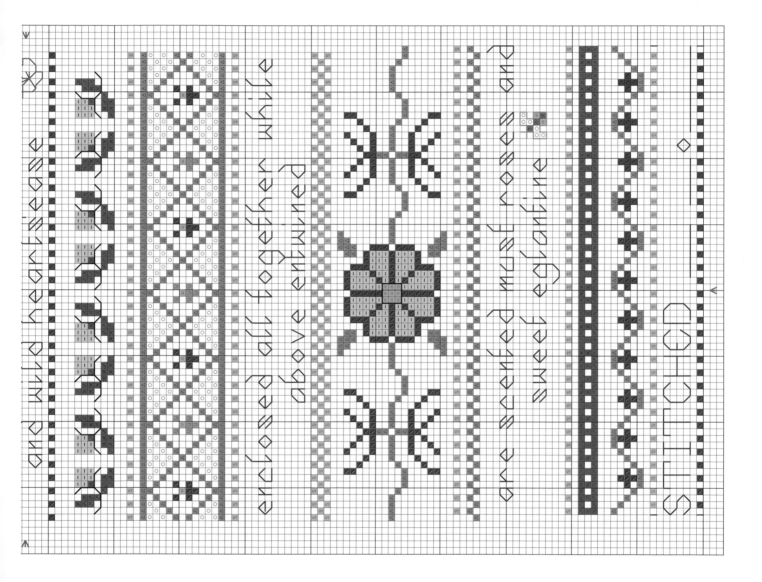

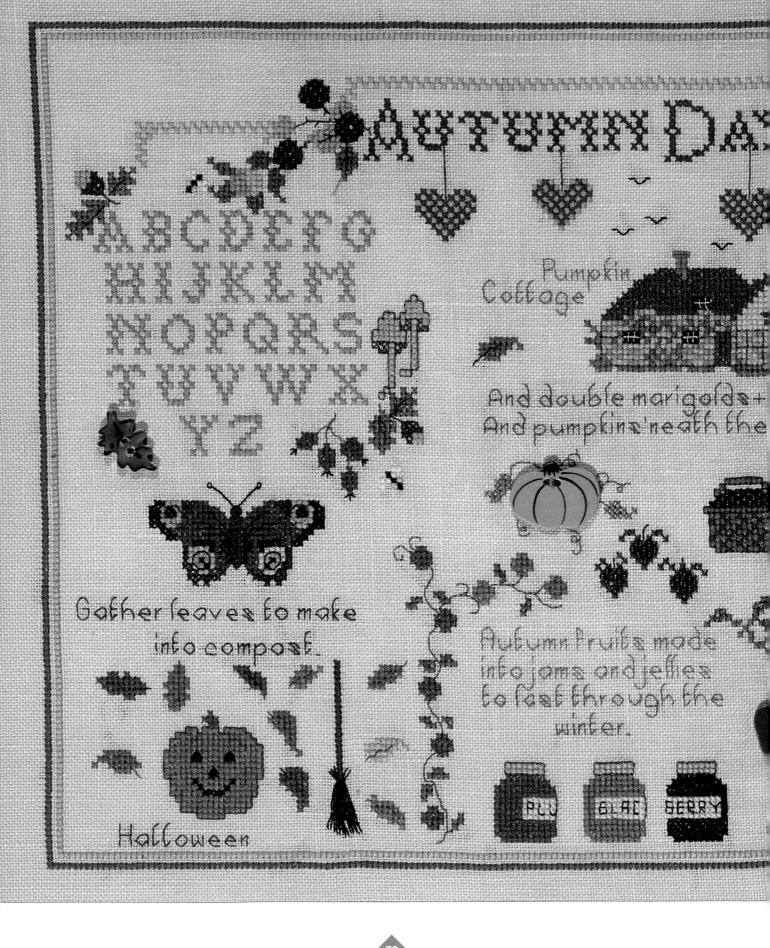

AUTUMN DA

Pumpkin
Cottage

And double marigolds +
And pumpkins 'neath the

Gather leaves to make
into compost.

Autumn fruits made
into jams and jellies
to last through the
winter.

Halloween

PLU GLAC BERRY

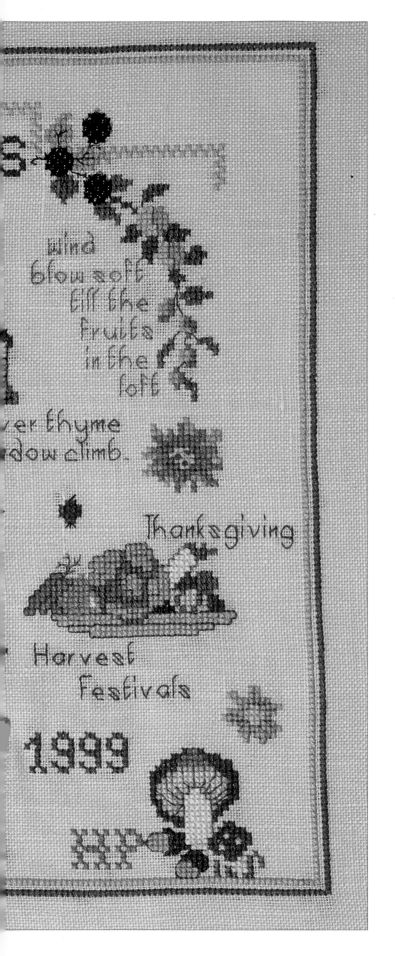

AUTUMN DAYS

This sampler is the third seasonal sampler in the book to be based on the traditional spot samplers. In this design I wanted to evoke the golden days of autumn with blackberries in the hedgerows, toadstools, harvest and falling leaves, using the warm earth tones we always associate with this season. There are many motifs in this main sampler which could be used for smaller pieces of work. You could also widen the seasonal colour range to include brighter yellows and reds.

> **Finished size: 13½ x 10½in (34 x 27cm)**
> **Stitch count: 149 x 195**

- ◆ **26 x 20in (66 x 51cm) 28 count linen in cream**
- ◆ **DMC stranded cottons as listed in the key**
- ◆ **Size 26 tapestry needle**
- ◆ **Seed beads in black and red**
- ◆ **Beading needle**
- ◆ **Mill Hill buttons (optional) – oak leaf, pumpkin and apple**

1 Find the centre of the fabric and begin stitching here over two threads of linen following the chart on page 72/73, using two strands of stranded cotton for the cross stitch and one for the French knots, backstitch and outlining. Use the Lettering Library to stitch your initials and date. Use an embroidery frame if you wish.

2 When the embroidery is complete, add the red beads to the raspberries using the beading needle and matching thread. Sew a mixture of red and black beads onto the blackberries with black thread. Add the buttons if you are using them or stitch their motifs from the chart instead.

3 Press the work carefully, avoiding the beads and buttons, and frame (see Techniques on page 125).

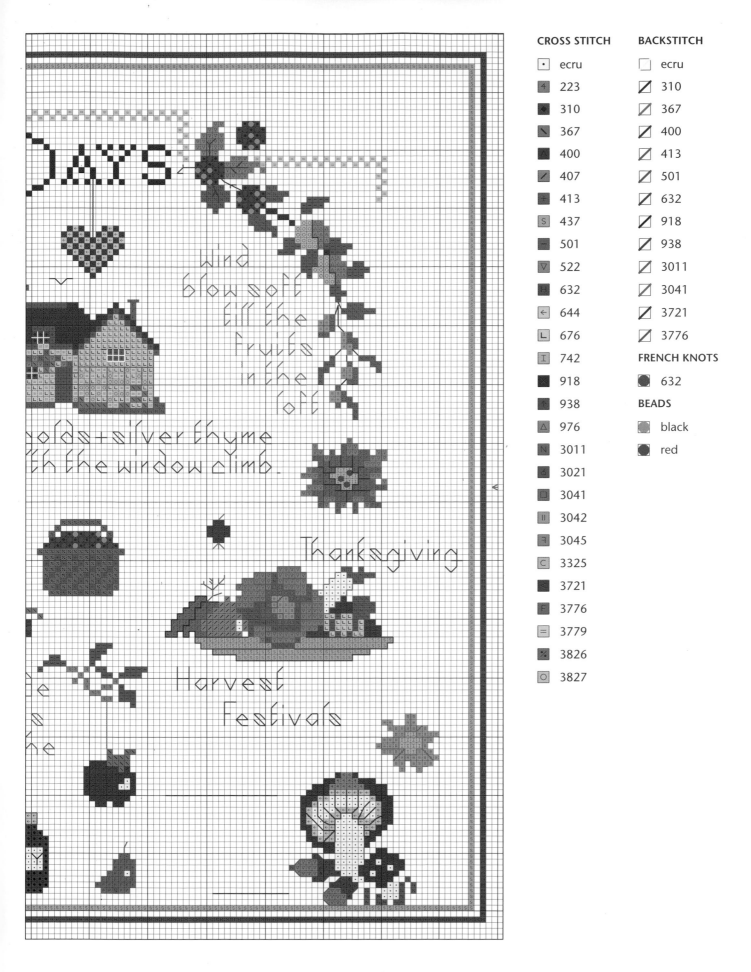

CROSS STITCH

·	ecru
4	223
◆	310
\	367
▲	400
/	407
+	413
S	437
–	501
▽	522
H	632
←	644
L	676
I	742
⊠	918
↑	938
△	976
N	3011
6	3021
▯	3041
II	3042
⊐	3045
C	3325
◣	3721
F	3776
=	3779
⁒	3826
○	3827

BACKSTITCH

☐	ecru
⟋	310
⟋	367
⟋	400
⟋	413
⟋	501
⟋	632
⟋	918
⟋	938
⟋	3011
⟋	3041
⟋	3721
⟋	3776

FRENCH KNOTS

| ● | 632 |

BEADS

| ○ | black |
| ● | red |

PUMPKIN PILLOW

This small pillow (shown opposite) uses the heart and pumpkin motifs from the Autumn Days Sampler. It combines several different crafts – cross stitch, patchwork and quilting – but each step is quite simple. The pillow could be filled with hops or herbs.

Finished size: 9in (23cm) square approximately

- ◆ **12in (30.5cm) square of 28 count linen in sand**
- ◆ **DMC stranded cottons from the main key**
- ◆ **15in (38cm) piece of novelty print cotton fabric with an autumn theme**
- ◆ **½yd (0.5m) of check cotton fabric in an autumn colour (rust or orange)**
- ◆ **10in (25cm) square of cream calico**
- ◆ **12in (30.5cm) piece of novelty print cotton fabric**
- ◆ **Cream sewing or quilting cotton**
- ◆ **10in (25cm) square of Bondaweb**
- ◆ **Nine 3in (7.5cm) square paper templates**
- ◆ **10in (25.4cm) piece of 4oz polyester wadding**
- ◆ **Polyester filling**
- ◆ **Mill Hill bee button and sweet corn button (optional)**
- ◆ **Two red-and-beige check ribbon bows**

To do the cross stitch

1 Cut the square of sand linen into four pieces 2½ x 2in (6 x 5cm). Take the first piece and finding the centre, begin stitching here over two fabric threads following the check heart motif on the Autumn Days Sampler chart on pages 72/73, using two strands of stranded cotton for the cross stitch.

2 When the cross stitching is complete, fray the edge of the linen by removing six threads from each side. Stitch and fray the other three pieces of linen and then iron Bondaweb onto the back of each piece, following the manufacturer's instructions.

3 Next, cut a 4in (10cm) square of sand linen and finding the centre, stitch the pumpkin motif from the Autumn Days Sampler chart, using two strands of stranded cotton for the cross stitch.

To do the patchwork

1 Cut four 4in (10cm) squares of rust check cotton and four 4in (10cm) squares of novelty fabric.

2 Take the four frayed-edge heart cross-stitched squares and iron one each in the centre of the four check cotton squares (see photograph right).

3 Take the nine 3in (7.5cm) square paper templates and place on the centre of each fabric square (including the linen pumpkin square), tacking round them to make patchwork squares. Position the nine squares as in the photograph and assemble by over-sewing the edges together. Remove all tacking.

To do the quilting

1 Sandwich the piece of wadding between the patchwork top and a square of calico and tack through the layers from the centre outwards to form a cross. Then using cream sewing or quilting cotton, quilt round each square just inside the seam line (see Stitch Library page 125).

2 Quilt round the cross stitch pumpkin. You can quilt as much or as little of the rest of the design as you wish – the printed fabric you have chosen may suggest obvious quilting lines. Sew on the bee and sweet corn buttons if you are using them.

To make up the pillow

1 Cut a piece of novelty print fabric 2in (5cm) larger than the pillow top and place right sides together with the patchwork piece. Sew round three sides of the pillow, then trim the seams, clip the corners and turn right side out.

2 Stuff the pillow with polyester filling and add hops or herbs if you wish. Sew up the remaining side and stitch two check ribbon bows to the top.

Projects inspired by the Autumn Days Sampler: the pumpkin pillow, sampler bell pull, hanging apple decoration, berry basket picture and scissors keeper

SAMPLER BELL PULL

This decoration (shown on page 75) would look good in a country kitchen. It uses motifs from the Autumn Days Sampler, showing how easy it is to create a fresh design.

- 21in (53cm) length of 2¼in (5.75cm) wide Aida band in oatmeal with cream edge
- DMC stranded cottons from the main key
- Seed beads in black and red
- Beading needle
- Mill Hill apple button and gold bee charm – both optional (see Suppliers page 127)
- Two bell pull ends

1 Find the centre of the band and begin stitching here from the Autumn Days Sampler chart (see chart on pages 72/73) and using the photograph on page 75 as a guide to the layout. Work over one block, using two strands of stranded cotton for the cross stitch and one for the backstitch.

2 Stitch outwards from the centre and when complete sew on the apple button, beads and charm.

3 Turn the ends of the band under and hem with matching sewing cotton, then attach the bell pull ends.

HANGING APPLE DECORATION

This decoration (shown on page 75) uses the apple motif from the Autumn Days Sampler (see chart on pages 72/73). You could make several and hang them together.

- 3½in (9cm) square of 28 count linen in sand
- DMC stranded cottons from the main key
- 3in (7.5cm) square of Bondaweb
- Two 5in (13cm) squares of red-and-beige check cotton fabric
- Red sewing cotton
- 5in (13cm) square of 2oz wadding
- 7in (18cm) length of brown garden twine
- Reel of cream crochet cotton

1 Find the centre of the linen and begin stitching over two threads following the main chart and using two strands of stranded cotton for the cross stitch.

2 When the stitching is complete, fray the edges of the linen by drawing fourteen threads away from each side. Iron a square of Bondaweb onto the back.

3 Iron the cross stitch design onto one piece of the check fabric. Take the other piece of fabric and with right sides together, sew round three sides, trimming the seams and clipping the corners. Turn out to the right side and insert the piece of wadding, then fold in the fourth side and slipstitch closed.

4 Using cream stranded cotton, quilt along the four edges ¼in (5mm) inside the seam line (see Stitch Library page 124). Using a large needle, tie four strands of cream crochet cotton in the corners to make a big knot and attach garden twine to the back for hanging.

BERRY BASKET PICTURE

This tiny picture (shown on page 75) uses the basket of berries motif from the Autumn Days Sampler. Stitch from the centre of a 4in (10cm) square of cream 28 count linen over two fabric threads following the main chart, using two strands for the cross stitch and one for outlining. Sew on black and red seed beads then iron a piece of Vilene onto the back. Trim to fit a frame with a 1¾in (4.5cm) square aperture.

AUTUMN FRUITS SCISSORS KEEPER

This project (shown on page 75) uses the yellow fruits motif from the Autumn Days Sampler (chart pages 72/73). You will need two pieces of cream 28 count linen 3in (7.5cm) square. Stitch from the centre of one of the squares, using two strands of stranded cotton for the cross stitch. Sew on a small gold bee charm, then follow steps 3 and 4 on page 22 for making up the scissors keeper and making a 12in (30cm) length of green and peach twisted cord. Stitch the cord all round, with a hanging loop in the top right corner.

THOMAS TUSSER SAMPLER

This sampler was designed because I wanted to have my own antique-looking sampler that wasn't actually a reproduction (see page 79). I chose the natural linen fabric for its aged quality and used the lovely quotation from Thomas Tusser's book published in 1580 *Five Hundred Pointes of Good Husbandrie*. The layout is that of a typical 'house and garden' sampler with its alphabets, verse, picture, spot motifs and border.

Finished size: 10½ x 14¼in (26.5 x 36cm)
Stitch count: 183 x 138

- ◆ 20 x 28in (51 x 71cm) 28 count linen in natural
- ◆ DMC stranded cottons as listed in the key
- ◆ Size 26 tapestry needle
- ◆ Small insect charm (optional–see Suppliers page 127)

1 Find the centre of the fabric and begin stitching here over two threads of linen following the chart on pages 80/81, using two strands of stranded cotton for the cross stitch and one strand for the backstitch and outlining. Use an embroidery frame if you wish.

2 Add your initials and date using page 119 of the Lettering Library. When complete, sew on the insect charm (if using one) where indicated by the black dot.

3 Finally, press the sampler carefully and frame (see Techniques page 125).

MINIATURE SAMPLER

This tiny sampler uses a few elements from the main Thomas Tusser Sampler (see page 79).

- ◆ 3 x 5in (7.5 x 13cm) 28 count linen in raw linen
- ◆ DMC stranded cottons from the main key
- ◆ 3 x 5in (7.5 x 13cm) piece of Vilene
- ◆ Wooden frame with 1½ x 2¼in (3.8 x 5.7cm) aperture

1 Find the centre of the fabric and begin stitching here over two threads of the linen fabric, following the main Thomas Tusser chart (see pages 80/81) and using the photograph on page 78 as a guide to the position of the sampler elements. Use two strands of stranded cotton for all the cross stitch and one strand for the backstitch.

2 When the stitching is complete, add your own initials and date worked out from the alphabet and numbers charted on page 119.

3 Press the work and iron the Vilene onto the back, according to the manufacturer's instructions. Trim and frame to finish.

THOMAS TUSSER KEY KEEPER

This charming little key keeper (pictured on page 78) features a floral design from the main Thomas Tusser Sampler and could be used to keep the key of an antique chest or bureau.

- ◆ Two 3in (7.5cm) squares of 28 count linen in raw linen
- ◆ DMC stranded cottons from the main key
- ◆ 18in (46cm) length of twisted cord in peach and green
- ◆ Gold key charm (optional)
- ◆ Sewing cotton to match linen
- ◆ Small amount of polyester filling

1 Find the centre of one of the pieces of linen and begin stitching the yellow flower motif here from the main chart on pages 80/81 using two strands of stranded cotton for the cross stitch. Add a cross stitch border line around the edge of the design in mustard

(782). When the stitching is complete, sew on the key charm if you are using it.

2 Take the second piece of linen and place it right sides together with the embroidered piece. Stitch round three sides close to the mustard cross stitch border, then trim the edges, clip the corners and turn right side out. Stuff the key keeper firmly with polyester filling and sew up the fourth side.

3 Make the twisted cord (see Techniques page 126) and sew it all the way round, making a loop at the top left-hand corner.

STRAWBERRY PINCUSHION

This would make a special gift for someone who enjoys needlework. It combines simple elements from the main Thomas Tusser Sampler into a new design (see picture opposite). Why not chose other motifs and combine them in an original design of your own?

- ◆ **5in (13cm) square of 14 count Floba fabric**
- ◆ **DMC stranded cottons as in the key**
- ◆ **Wooden base pincushion (see Suppliers page 127)**

1 Find the centre of the fabric and begin stitching here following the main chart on pages 80/81 and using the photograph opposite as a guide to the design layout. Use two strands of stranded cotton for the cross stitch over two threads of fabric and one strand for the outlining. Use a flexihoop if you wish.

2 When the stitching is complete, press the embroidery carefully and mount in the pincushion lid according to the manufacturer's instructions.

The attractive Thomas Tusser Sampler and the spin-off projects based on its many motifs: a miniature sampler, key keeper and pincushion

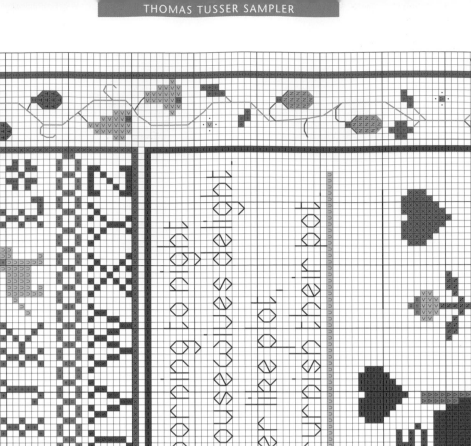

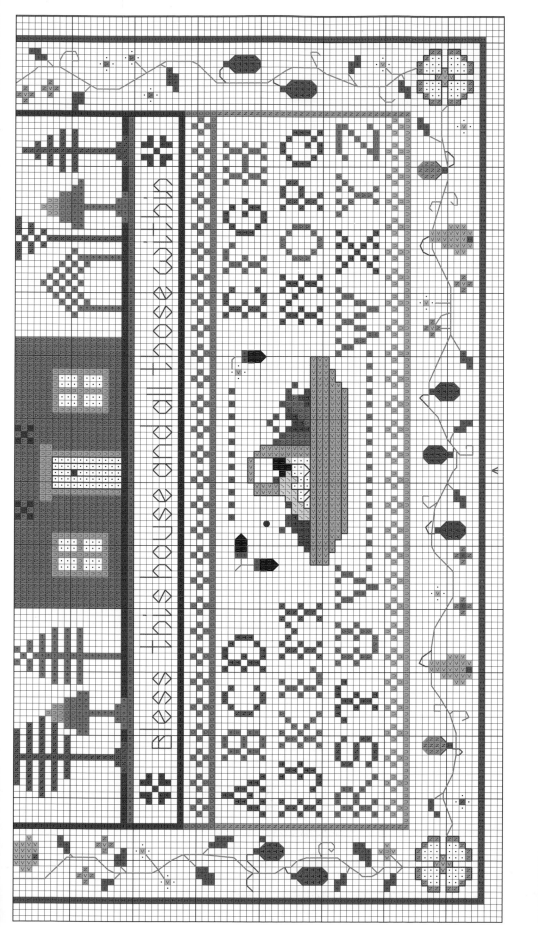

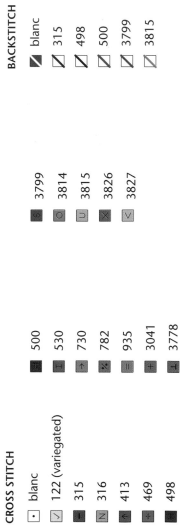

CROSS STITCH

·	blanc
⌄	122 (variegated)
▮	315
Z	316
◄	413
+	469
▬	498

▦	500	S	3799
⊢	530	O	3814
↑	730	U	3815
⁒	782	X	3826
=	935	V	3827
+	3041		
⌐	3778		

BACKSTITCH

◥	blanc
◿	315
◥	498
◿	500
◿	3799
◿	3815

HALLOWE'EN SAMPLER

This modern sampler, with its bright orange and yellow motifs contrasting well against the unusual tan-coloured linen, is for all those who enjoy celebrating Hallowe'en with all its traditional spookiness and tricks or treats. Other designs developed from this sampler could make great Hallowe'en gifts if you don't have time to stitch the whole sampler before the scariest night of the year arrives.

Finished size: 3¾ x 7¾in (9.5 x 19.5cm)
Stitch count: 110 x 54

◆ 8 x 16in (20 x 40.5cm) 28 count linen in tan
◆ DMC stranded cottons as listed in the key
◆ Size 26 tapestry needle
◆ Mill Hill buttons (optional) – black cat, white star

1 Find the centre of the fabric and begin stitching here over two threads of linen following the chart on page 85 and using an embroidery frame if you wish. Use two strands of stranded cotton for the cross stitch and French knots and one strand for the backstitch and outlining. Use the Lettering Library to stitch your initials and date.

2 When the stitching is complete, sew on the buttons if you are using them or work the motifs from the chart instead. Use Algerian eye stitch (see Stitch Library page 123) for both large white stars.

3 Press the sampler carefully, avoiding any buttons used and then frame (see Techniques page 125).

The very modern Hallowe'en Sampler with a fun owl picture and spooky card

OWL PICTURE

This picture (see page 83) would make a lovely present for a child with its old-fashioned storybook appearance. It uses the owl and moon motif from the main Hallowe'en Sampler, plus a sprinkling of 'stars' worked in star stitch. I have worked it on a dramatic black but you could use any dark linen or Aida fabric.

◆ **6in (15cm) square of 14 count Aida in black**
◆ **DMC stranded cottons from the main key**
◆ **6in (15cm) square of Vilene**
◆ **Pine frame with 3in (7.5cm) square aperture**

1 Find the centre of the fabric and begin stitching here over one block following the owl and moon motif from the main chart on page 85. Use two strands of stranded cotton for the cross stitch and one strand for the outlining and star stitches (see Stitch Library page 125). You could use a flexihoop if you wish.

2 When the stitching is complete, press the work and iron Vilene onto the back according to the manufacturer's instructions.

3 Trim to fit and frame to finish.

HALLOWE'EN CARD

This little card (see page 83) is quick to make and fun to send. I have used a pumpkin button on mine but you could stitch the pumpkin motif from the main Hallowe'en Sampler instead if you prefer.

◆ **4 x 6in (10 x 15cm) 28 count linen in tan**
◆ **DMC stranded cottons from the main key**
◆ **4 x 6in (10 x 15cm) piece of Vilene**
◆ **Mill Hill pumpkin button (optional)**
◆ **Ready-made card mount 2 x 2¾in (5 x 7cm) aperture**

1 Find the centre of the fabric and begin stitching here over two threads using various motifs from the main chart on page 85 (see photograph on page 83) and the alphabet on page 120. Use two strands of thread for the cross stitch and one for the backstitch.

2 When the stitching is complete, sew on the pumpkin button if you are using it or stitch the motif from the chart instead. Press and then iron the Vilene onto the back of the embroidery.

3 To finish, mount the design in the card (see Techniques page 126).

You could decorate a plain frame with star or moon rubber stamps for this picture.

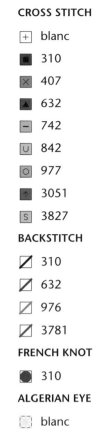

CROSS STITCH

+	blanc
■	310
✕	407
▲	632
−	742
U	842
○	977
↑	3051
S	3827

BACKSTITCH

⁄	310
⁄	632
⁄	976
⁄	3781

FRENCH KNOT

●	310

ALGERIAN EYE

▨	blanc

THANKSGIVING SAMPLER

This attractive sampler shows its American influences in both title and style. I found the subject matter very inspiring to design for and enjoyed discovering new colour combinations. The lovely Caron thread which I used for part of the stitching creates interesting effects and the subtle, warm colours helped to produce the 'country' style I was seeking.

> **Finished size: 9½ x 7in (24 x 18cm)**
> **Stitch count: 135 x 99**

◆ 18 x 14in (46 x 35.5cm) 28 count linen in cream
◆ DMC stranded cottons as listed in the key
◆ Caron Wildflowers thread Painted Desert
◆ Size 26 tapestry needle
◆ Bird button (optional, see Suppliers page 127)

1 Find the centre of the fabric and begin stitching here over two threads of linen following the chart on pages 88/89, using an embroidery frame if you wish. Use two strands of stranded cotton for the cross stitch and one strand for the backstitch and outlining. Use only one strand of the Caron thread throughout. Use the Lettering Library to stitch your initials and date.

2 When the stitching is complete, sew on the bird button with matching thread if you are using it. In this sampler the button is an extra, sewn on top of the stitched basket and can be omitted if preferred.

3 Press the work carefully and then frame (see Techniques page 125).

GREETING CARDS

These three attractive little greeting cards use motifs from the main Thanksgiving Sampler and are very quick to stitch.

For each card
◆ 4 x 6in (10 x 15cm) 28 count linen in cream
◆ Stranded cottons from the main key

◆ 3 x 5in (7.5 x 13cm) lightweight iron-on Vilene
◆ One blue bird button for the basket card (optional, see Suppliers page 127)
◆ Card mount in textured cream with 2 x 2¾in (5 x 7cm) aperture

1 Stitch the first design of your choice following the main chart on pages 88/89 and using a flexihoop if you wish. Use two strands of stranded cotton for the cross stitch and one strand for the backstitch and outlining over two threads of linen. Use the alphabet on page 120 for any lettering required. Each card has a simple cross stitch border – see photograph opposite for design details.

2 When the stitching is complete, add the bird button to the basket design at this point if using it. Press the work and then iron a piece of Vilene onto the back of the embroidery following the manufacturer's instructions.

3 Make up a card according to the instructions on page 126. Continue on to complete your next card in the same way.

The beautifully coloured Thanksgiving Sampler, with three charming cards that feature some of its motifs. These are perfect for many occasions, for example, you could stitch the jug of flowers card as a get well card or for a birthday

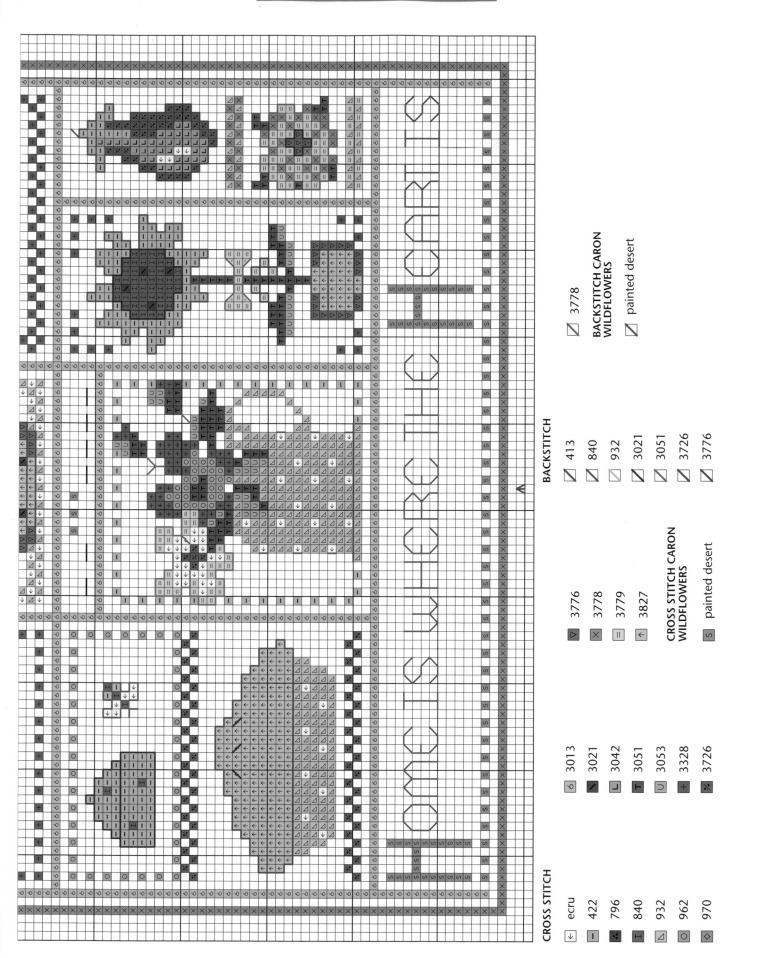

CROSS STITCH

↓	ecru
I	422
⠿	796
H	840
△	932
O	962
◇	970

⟡	3013
◢	3021
L	3042
T	3051
U	3053
+	3328
⧆	3726

▷	3776
×	3778
‖	3779
←	3827

CROSS STITCH CARON WILDFLOWERS

| S | painted desert |

BACKSTITCH

⟋	413
⟋	840
⟋	932
⟋	3021
⟋	3051
⟋	3726
⟋	3776

| ⟋ | 3778 |

BACKSTITCH CARON WILDFLOWERS

| ⟋ | painted desert |

Red Fox Farm Sampler

This sampler began with the words I saw hand-painted on a wobbly sign at the end of a lane near my home. I have never seen the actual farm but I liked the sound of its name. On subsequent autumn walks (with camera and sketchbook), I gathered images of farms, ploughed fields, cows, hens and geese, and the design developed from there. The fox himself is a regular visitor to our garden. The design evolved as a traditional sampler layout with alphabet, numbers, picture and border. I liked the idea of the night sky forming a solid border around the central image.

Finished size: 11 x 10in (28 x 25.5cm)
Stitch count: 160 x 146

- **22 x 20in (56 x 51cm) 28 count Quaker cloth in cream**
- **DMC stranded cottons as listed in the key**
- **Size 26 tapestry needle**

1 Find the centre of the Quaker cloth fabric and begin stitching here over two fabric threads following the chart on pages 92/93. Use an embroidery frame to keep your work taut if you wish. Use the Lettering Library to stitch your initials and date. Use two strands of stranded cotton for all the cross stitch, except for the following:

For the birds in the sky and the silhouetted meadowsweet and grass behind the fox use two strands for the backstitch and cross stitch.

For the owl's, geese and hen's eyes use one strand and French knots (see Stitch Library page 124).

For the cow's tails use two strands and backstitch.

For the outlining use one strand.

2 When all the stitching is complete, press your embroidery and frame (see Techniques page 125).

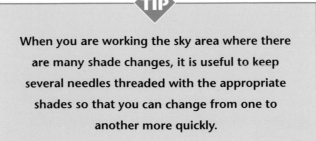

TIP

When you are working the sky area where there are many shade changes, it is useful to keep several needles threaded with the appropriate shades so that you can change from one to another more quickly.

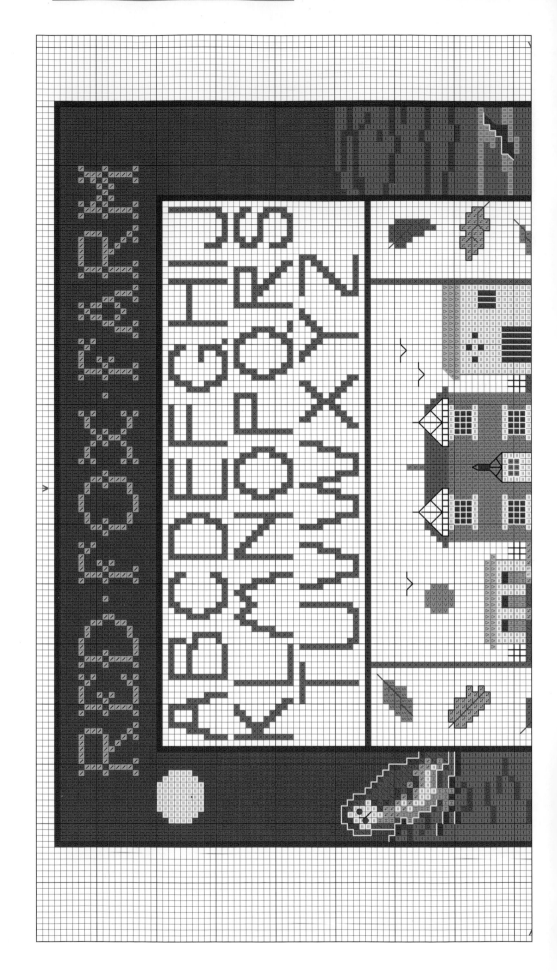

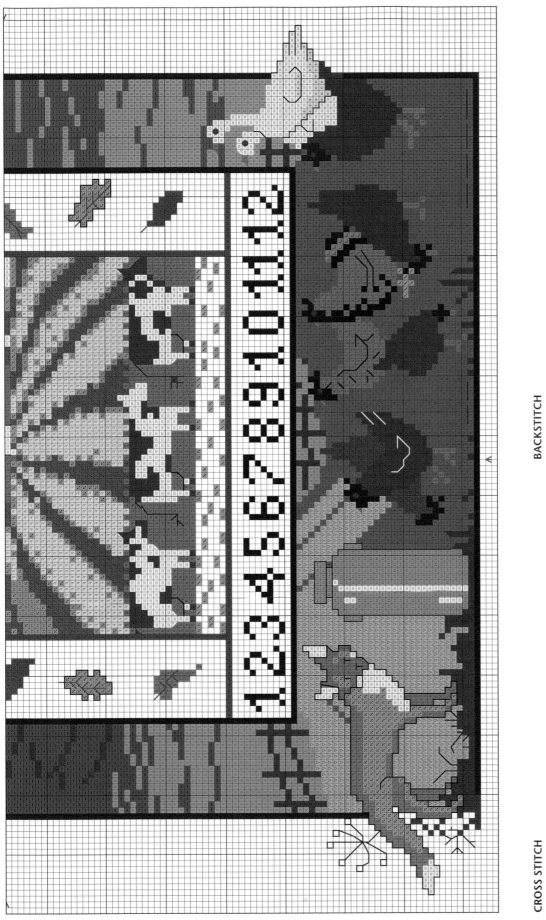

CROSS STITCH

=	ecru	
⊞	310	
I	312	
+	317	
▷	318	
=	334	
○	336	

⊞	347	
%	437	
⊞	918	
X	921	
⊞	939	
S	976	
▽	3021	

H	3023	
F	3033	
╱	3045	
↓	3743	
V	3778	
N	3790	
L	3814	

BACKSTITCH

☐	ecru
╱	310
╱	317
╱	918
╱	3021

FRENCH KNOT

●	310

WINTER'S TA[LE]

Mistletoe Cottage

There seems a
magic in the
very name of
CHRISTMAS

Here we come a-wassailing
Among the leaves ♫♪
so green

WINTER'S TALE

This design is the final sampler in the series of seasonal spot samplers in this book. I wanted to explore an old-fashioned mid-winter feeling and create a wintry atmosphere in this design, as well as using Christmas themes. There are several gift ideas that have been inspired by the elements in this sampler and lots of seasonal decorations and gift tags that you could make.

> **Finished size: 13½ x 10½in (34 x 26.5cm)**
> **Stitch count: 147 x 193**

- ◆ 26 x 20in (66 x 51cm) 28 count linen in grey
- ◆ DMC stranded cottons as listed in the key
- ◆ Madeira Glamour thread 2442
- ◆ Size 26 tapestry needle
- ◆ Mill Hill buttons (optional) – 2 lanterns, 1 gingerbread man and 1 star
- ◆ Snowflake charms (optional)

1 Find the centre of the fabric and begin stitching here over two threads of linen, using an embroidery frame if you wish, and following the chart given on pages 100/101. Use two strands of stranded cotton for the cross stitch and French knots and one strand for the backstitch and outlining. Work the silver stars in Algerian eye stitch (see Stitch Library page 123) using two strands of light silver. Use the Lettering Library (pages 119/120) to stitch your initials and date.

2 When the stitching is complete, sew on the buttons with matching thread if you have chosen to use them or stitch the motifs from the chart instead.

3 Finally, press the work carefully avoiding any buttons you have used, and frame (see Techniques page 125).

PATCHWORK CUSHION

This 9½in (24cm) square cushion combines some of my favourite crafts, including cross stitch, appliqué, patchwork and quilting. It uses motifs from the main Winter's Tale Sampler (chart pages 100/101). You could make a padded heart to hang from one of the buttons, or a stitched gift tag to accompany this cushion.

◆ Seven 5in (13cm) squares of patterned flannel fabric – 3 dark blues, 3 dark reds, 1 dark green

◆ Two 5in (13cm) squares of cream calico

◆ Four small pieces of patterned blue, red and green flannel for the appliqué

◆ 12in (30.5cm) square of 28 count linen in natural

◆ Stranded cottons from the main key

◆ 10in (25.5cm) square of Bondaweb

◆ White, dark red and dark blue sewing cotton

◆ Quilting thread in cream, red and blue

◆ 12in (30.5cm) square of 4oz polyester wadding

◆ 12in (30.5cm) square of calico for backing the quilted front of the cushion

◆ 12in (30.5cm) square of red flannel for backing

◆ 9in (23cm) cushion pad

◆ Buttons – Mill Hill Christmas tree and white star and Debbie Mumm winged heart in red (see Suppliers)

◆ Thin card templates of: a 3in (7.5cm) square (A); a star (B); a large heart (C); a small heart (D) (see page 122)

To do the cross stitch

1 Make the square (A), star (B) and heart (C and D) templates by tracing the shapes onto thin card and cutting out. Using the square template cut out one dark green, three dark blue, three dark red flannel squares and two calico squares, leaving a ¼in (5mm) seam allowance on all pieces.

2 Take a 3½in (9cm) square of the linen and stitch the sheep motif from the main chart. Iron Bondaweb onto the back. Place the large heart template (C) on the linen, draw round it and cut out. Iron this heart onto a red flannel square, then blanket stitch round the edge of the heart with grey stranded cotton (see Stitch Library page 124). Repeat this process with the

lantern motif, applying it to a different red flannel square. Repeat again with the holly, applying it to a dark green flannel square (see photograph opposite).

3 Take two pieces of linen, about 2½in (6.5cm) square, and stitch a red berry motif from the chart in the centre of each. Iron Bondaweb onto the backs. Place the small heart template (D) onto each of these linen pieces, draw round and cut out the shapes. Iron one onto a piece of red flannel and one onto a piece of green, then blanket stitch round the edge of the hearts with grey stranded cotton.

4 Iron Bondaweb onto the backs of the red and green flannel squares in turn and use the large heart template (C) to cut out the shapes. Iron each onto a calico square, blanket stitching round the hearts with matching thread.

5 Take small pieces of red and blue flannel and iron Bondaweb onto the backs, then draw round the star template (B) and cut out the shape from both pieces. Iron the blue star onto a dark red flannel square, then iron the red onto a blue flannel square. Top stitch in matching thread.

To do the patchwork

1 Take the nine square templates and fold the decorated fabric squares round them and tack in place. Arrange the patches as in the photograph,

You could make the patchwork top of this cushion into a folk art wall hanging instead by completing all the stages up to the quilting and then turning in the edges and hemming them. Hang it by garden twine loops from a garden cane or rustic twig.

The spin-off projects from the Winter's Tale Sampler: the patchwork cushion, country heart Christmas decorations, fabric gift tags, padded heart gift tag and Christmas card gift tags

oversewing the edges together. Use dark cotton to join dark edges and light cotton where light joins dark. When the patchwork is complete add the buttons if you are using them.

2 Press the patchwork carefully and trim excess fabric to reduce bulk.

To do the quilting

1 Sandwich the wadding between the patchwork top and the calico backing and tack in place, working out from the centre and forming a cross.

2 Using the relevant coloured quilting thread, quilt round the squares just inside the seam (see Stitch Library page 125), and then around the heart and star shapes. Remove the tacking.

3 Take the red flannel backing and placing right sides together with the patchwork top, stitch round three sides. Trim the seams, clip the corners and turn the right way out. Insert the cushion pad, then sew up the fourth side.

COUNTRY HEART CHRISTMAS DECORATIONS

These charmingly rustic decorations (shown on page 97) could be used in many ways – to hang on the Christmas tree, to add to wreaths, or to attach to gifts. They use the robin and holly sprig motifs from the main Winter's Tale Sampler (see charts on pages 100/101).

For one heart

◆ 3in (7.5cm) square of 28 count linen in cream
◆ Two 7in (18cm) squares of red-and-cream or red-and-green check cotton fabric
◆ Stranded cottons from the main key
◆ One plain button
◆ 3in (7.5cm) square of Bondaweb
◆ Templates in thin card of the large heart (E) and small heart (F) (traced from page 122 and cut out)
◆ Polyester filling
◆ 12in (30.5cm) length of garden twine

1 Find the centre of the linen square and stitch either the robin or holly motif from the main chart here over two fabric threads, using two strands of stranded cotton for the cross stitch.

2 Iron the piece of Bondaweb onto the back. Then, using the small heart template (F), draw the shape onto the back and cut out.

3 Using the large heart template (E), cut out two hearts from the check fabric then iron the smaller heart onto one larger one and blanket stitch round the edge with matching thread (see Stitch Library page 124). Sew on the button.

4 With right sides together stitch the front and back hearts together leaving a small gap. Trim the seams, clip the curves and turn to the right side.

5 Stuff firmly with polyester filling then stitch up the small gap. Decorate with the twine stitched on at the top and tied in a bow.

> **TIP**
>
> You could use the heart template to make a pincushion instead, and perhaps fill it with bran which people used to put in their pincushions to keep their pins and needles sharp.

FABRIC GIFT TAGS

These unusual Christmas gift tags (see page 97) use the decorative alphabet from the Winter's Tale Sampler. You can easily change the name or message to one of your own or stitch different motifs from the chart.

For the Rosie tag

◆ 6 x 3½in (15 x 9cm) piece of 28 count linen in natural linen
◆ 6 x 3in (15 x 7.5cm) piece of red-and-green check cotton fabric
◆ 5½ x 1½in (14 x 4cm) piece of Bondaweb

- ◆ A thin card template 5¼ x 1¼in (13.3 x 3.1cm)
- ◆ 26in (66cm) length of twisted cord in dark blue, red and green
- ◆ Gold bell and little red bow to decorate

For the heart tag

- ◆ 3in (7.5cm) square of 32 count Belfast linen in raw linen
- ◆ 3in (7.5cm) square of red and green star pattern cotton fabric
- ◆ 3in (7.5cm) square of Bondaweb
- ◆ Thin card heart template (G) (traced from page 122 and cut out)
- ◆ 8in (20cm) length of twisted cord in red and blue

For both tags

- ◆ Stranded cottons from the main key
- ◆ Copydex glue

1 Work out on graph paper the name or message you wish to stitch from the main chart alphabet. 'Rosie' was stitched over two threads but if your lettering is lengthy you may have to work it over one thread, as the 'Merry Xmas' message was.

2 Find the centre of the piece of linen and begin stitching here using two strands of stranded cotton for the 'Rosie' cross stitch and one strand for the heart-shaped tag. When the name tag lettering is complete, add the holly on either side following the main chart.

3 Iron Bondaweb onto the back of the embroidery and trim to fit the relevant template (the rectangular one for 'Rosie' and the heart for the heart-shaped tag). Take the relevant piece of backing fabric and iron the design onto it, trimming to match.

4 Make the relevant twisted cord (see Techniques page 126) and glue it all the way round the tag leaving the spare length at the top left-hand corner of the 'Rosie' tag and at the top of the heart-shaped tag. Stitch this into a loop, forming the end into a tassel for the 'Rosie' tag. Attach the bells and bow.

PADDED HEART CHRISTMAS GIFT TAG

This tag (see page 97) could be used as a decoration for the Christmas tree as well as to give with a gift. It uses the holly motif from the Winter's Tale Sampler.

- ◆ Two 4in (10cm) squares of 28 count linen in natural linen
- ◆ Stranded cottons from the main key
- ◆ Thin card heart template (G) (see page 122)
- ◆ 15in (38cm) length of twisted cord in dark blue, red and green
- ◆ Small amount of polyester filling
- ◆ Copydex glue

1 Begin stitching from the centre of the first linen square over two fabric threads following the main chart on pages 100/101 and using two strands of stranded cotton for the cross stitch.

2 When the stitching is complete, draw round the heart template (G) onto the back of the embroidery. Take the backing fabric and with right sides together sew round the heart shape, leaving a small gap. Trim round the shape, clip the curves and turn the right way out.

3 Stuff the heart with a small amount of filling and sew up the gap. Make the twisted cord (see Techniques page 126) and glue around the edge, making a loop at the top.

CHRISTMAS CARD GIFT TAGS

These tags (shown on page 97) are quick to make, adding a special touch to gifts. They use motifs from the Winter's Tale Sampler. Stitch your first motif from the main chart on a 3in (7.5cm) square of cream 28 count linen over two fabric threads. Use two strands of stranded cotton for the cross stitch and one for the backstitch and outlining. When the embroidery is complete, iron a piece of Vilene onto the back, then make up into a ready-made 2in (5cm) square card with a circular aperture (see Techniques page 126).

CROSS STITCH

·	ecru
N	301
+	310
→	317
↑	340
U	347
I	437
▽	445
Z	500
II	501
H	730
←	742
◼	816
◀	930
∩	3023
□	3362
⊤	3721
=	3746
T	3826
S	3827

BACKSTITCH

□	ecru
⊘	301
⊘	310
⊘	317
⊘	340
⊘	500
⊘	501
⊘	730
⊘	816
⊘	930

BACKSTITCH

⊘	Madeira Glamour 2442

FRENCH KNOTS

□	ecru
●	310
●	347
●	501
▢	742

CROSS STITCH

⊙	Madeira Glamour 2442

COLD DECEMBER SAMPLER

This sampler was inspired by a set of Christmas buttons. I decided to use each one in its own small frame of matching colours and added a verse from an old poem by Sara Coleridge to create a Christmas atmosphere. Little samplers like this are very versatile as the simple motifs can be used on many small items. Any of the buttons could be replaced by stitching the motifs on the chart or by substituting with suitable motifs from other charts in the book.

Finished size: 8in (20cm) square
Stitch count: 99 x 94

- 12in (30.5cm) square of 28 count linen in cream
- DMC stranded cottons as listed in the key
- Size 26 tapestry needle
- Mill Hill buttons (optional, see Suppliers page 127) – snowman, gingerbread man and rocking horse

1 Find the centre of the fabric and begin stitching here over two threads of linen following the chart on page 104. Use an embroidery frame to keep your work taut if you wish. Use two strands of stranded cotton for the cross stitch and French knots, and one strand for the backstitch and outlining.

2 When the stitching is complete, sew on the decorative buttons with matching thread if you have chosen to use them, or alternatively stitch the motifs from the chart in their place.

3 Press the sampler carefully, avoiding any buttons used and then frame (see Techniques page 125).

The Cold December Sampler with its festive spin-off projects – three Christmas cards and a useful gift bag

CHRISTMAS CARDS

The decorative buttons which are used in the Cold December Sampler inspired the motifs for this set of cards. The motifs could be used in other ways, perhaps stitched in bands onto Christmas guest towels or as single motifs in the corners of napkins.

For all 3 cards

- Three 3 x 4in (8 x 10cm) pieces of 28 count linen in beige
- DMC stranded cottons from the main key
- Three 2in (5cm) squares of lightweight iron-on Vilene
- Three Christmas card blanks with 1½in (4.5cm) square apertures

1 Stitch the first motif of your choice over two threads of linen following the main chart, using cross stitch and two strands of thread throughout.

2 When the stitching is complete, iron a 2in (5cm) square of Vilene onto the back of the embroidery following the manufacturer's instructions. Make up into a card (see Techniques page 126).

TIP

Look out for inexpensive 'fun' Christmas jewellery to embellish Christmas samplers and decorations. Lovely little bells, parcels, candysticks and so on are great to dismantle and add to your stitching.

CROSS STITCH

- • ecru
- ▲ 310
- ▬ 347
- ◉ 433
- H 437
- + 520
- U 522
- = 3823

BACKSTITCH

- ▱ ecru
- ◿ 310
- ◿ 347
- ◿ 433
- ◿ 520

FRENCH KNOT

- ⬢ 310

ALGERIAN EYE

- ✳ 437

CHRISTMAS TREAT GIFT BAG

This bag (shown on page 102) would make a gift extra special. It could be filled with sweets or pot-pourri and hung on the tree.

- Two 14 x 10in (36.5 x 26.5cm) pieces of 32 count Belfast linen in natural
- Size 26 tapestry needle
- DMC stranded cottons as listed in the key
- Mill Hill snowman button (optional, see Suppliers page 127)
- 1yd (1m) of ¼in (5mm) red ribbon
- Gold bells or other Christmas decoration trimmings

1 Fold the first piece of linen in half vertically to find the middle, measure 2½in (6cm) up from the bottom, find the centre stitch on the fold and begin work here.

2 Stitch the design from the chart below using two strands of DMC stranded cotton for the cross stitch, French knots and the Algerian eye stitch (see Stitch Library page 123) and one strand for the backstitch. Sew on the snowman button with matching thread or stitch the charted motif in its place.

3 When the stitching is complete, count thirty-seven threads from the top stitching row and withdraw four threads. This is to thread the ribbon through. Count twenty threads further up again and withdraw three threads. Using antique hem stitch (see Stitch Library page 123), make a hem using one strand of red stranded cotton.

4 Take the second piece of fabric (the back of the bag), and withdraw four threads as for the ribbon row and three threads for the hemming, to match the front of the bag.

5 With right sides together sew up the sides and bottom. Press the seams and clip the corners. Turn the bag the right way out and thread the ribbon through the withdrawn row. Add the bells and pull up and tie.

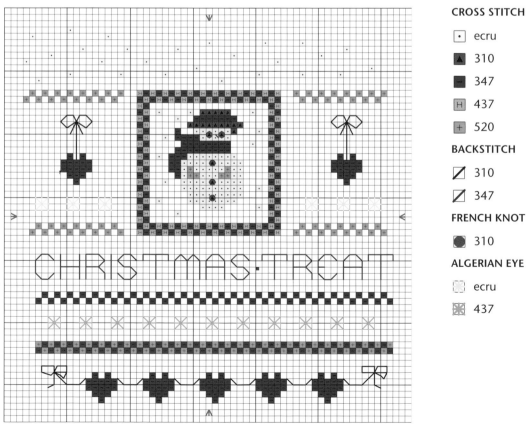

CROSS STITCH
- · ecru
- ▲ 310
- ■ 347
- H 437
- + 520

BACKSTITCH
- ⧄ 310
- ⧄ 347

FRENCH KNOT
- ● 310

ALGERIAN EYE
- ⬚ ecru
- ✳ 437

WINTER GARDEN SAMPLER

I decided to use mid-winter as a theme as it was so different from usual garden embroideries that are full of flowers and bright colours. I love images of snow and it was interesting trying to create the frosty feel of the winter garden, exploring different techniques in doing so. The band sampler is one of the oldest types of sampler but the colour, style and content of this one make it one of the more modern designs in the book.

> **Finished size: 4½ x 8in (11 x 20cm)**
> **Stitch count: 119 x 65**

◆ 10 x 16in (25.5 x 40.5cm) 31 count Belfast in raw linen
◆ DMC stranded cottons as in the key
◆ Size 26 tapestry needle

1 Find the centre of the fabric and begin stitching here over two threads of linen, using an embroidery frame if you wish, and following the chart on page 108. Use two strands of DMC stranded cotton for the cross stitch and French knots and one strand for the backstitch and outlining, except for the following:

For the star stitches use one strand (see Stitch Library page 125).
For the Algerian eye stitches use two strands (see Stitch Library page 123).
For the berry stems use two strands and backstitch.
For the white cross stitch in the band with the holly use one strand.
For the proverb 'If Candlemas Day…' use one strand over one thread of linen.

2 Work outwards from the centre until all the stitching is complete, then press the embroidery carefully and frame (see Techniques page 125).

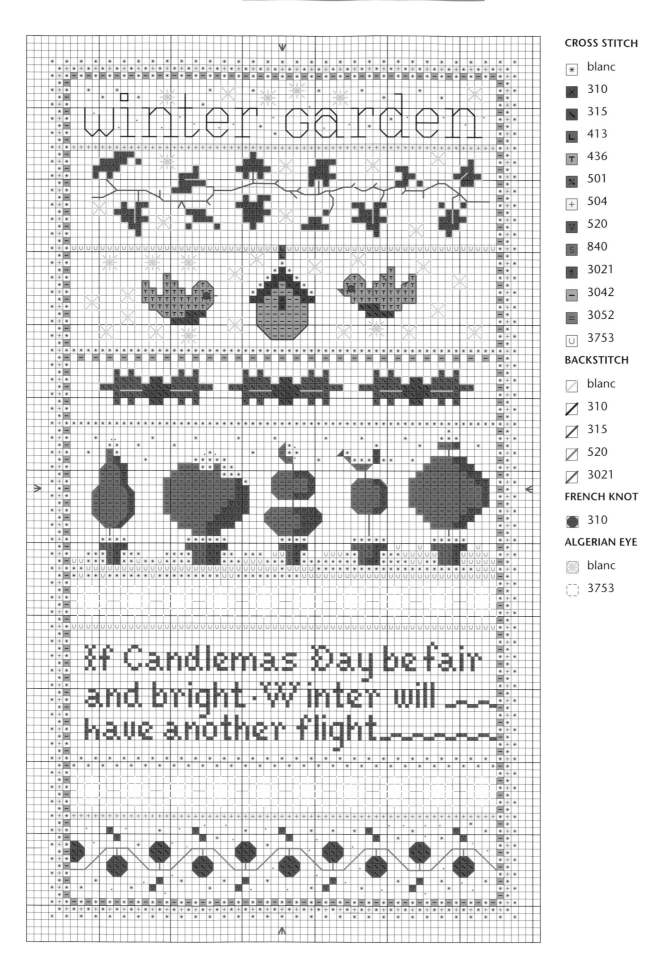

CROSS STITCH

✳	blanc
✕	310
◣	315
L	413
T	436
⁒	501
+	504
▽	520
S	840
↑	3021
−	3042
═	3052
U	3753

BACKSTITCH

⧄	blanc
⧄	310
⧄	315
⧄	520
⧄	3021

FRENCH KNOT

●	310

ALGERIAN EYE

✸	blanc
⬚	3753

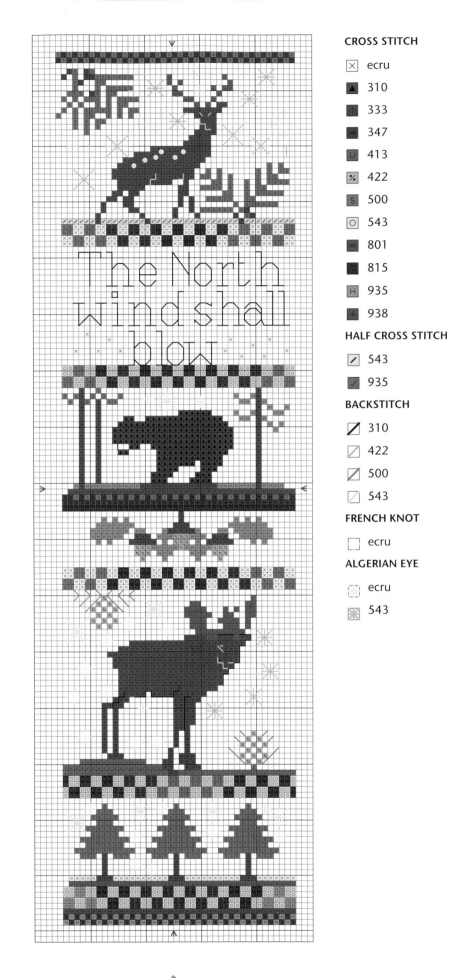

CROSS STITCH

⊠ ecru
▲ 310
⬛ 333
— 347
U 413
% 422
S 500
○ 543
⬛ 801
▼ 815
H 935
+ 938

HALF CROSS STITCH

⟋ 543
⟋ 935

BACKSTITCH

⟋ 310
⟋ 422
⟋ 500
⟋ 543

FRENCH KNOT

☐ ecru

ALGERIAN EYE

⬚ ecru
✳ 543

ANIMALS OF THE NORTH SAMPLER

This sampler was inspired by the great northern woods of America which have always fascinated me. I love American textiles and the images they contain, so this sampler is my version of a truly American subject. Although designed along basic band sampler lines, the individual elements can easily be adapted to make smaller decorative pieces.

> **Finished size: 3 x 11in (7.5 x 28cm)**
> **Stitch count: 156 x 42**

- ◆ 6 x 22in (15 x 56cm) 28 count linen in tan
- ◆ DMC stranded cottons as listed in the key
- ◆ Size 26 tapestry needle

1 Find the centre of the fabric and begin stitching here over two threads of linen following the chart on page 109 and using an embroidery frame if you wish. Use two strands of stranded cotton for the cross stitch and one strand for the backstitch and outlining. For the star stitches use one strand (see Stitch Library page 125).
For the markings on the deer use one strand and French knots (see Stitch Library page 124).

2 Work outwards from the centre until all the stitching is complete, then press the work carefully and frame (see Techniques page 125).

The bold and festive Animals of the North Sampler with its two spin-off projects: the fir trees Christmas bow and two hand-made Christmas cards

FIR TREES CHRISTMAS BOW

This country-style Christmas decoration (shown on page 111) uses the fir trees from the Animals of the North Sampler and could be used in many different ways – with a length of ribbon to hang up Christmas cards, with a rustic basket filled with greenery and candles or attached to a swag or wreath.

◆ 16in (41cm) length of 2in (5cm) wide Aida band in cream with cream edge
◆ DMC stranded cottons from the main key
◆ 16 x 2in (41 x 5cm) piece of Bondaweb
◆ 16 x 2in (41 x 5cm) piece red-and-beige check cotton lining fabric

1 Find the centre of the Aida band and begin stitching here over one block following the main chart on page 109 and using two strands of stranded cotton for the cross stitch. Work along one side of the band and then the other. Note that the borders along the top and bottom vary slightly from the main chart, using sand (422) instead of white and with a single line only along the top (see photograph on page 111).

2 Stitch fourteen trees then cut away the spare band from each end, leaving enough to make small seams. Using one of these cut-offs, cross stitch a 3in (7.5cm) length of the bottom border checks only.

3 Iron Bondaweb onto the back of the bow, according to the manufacturer's instructions, then take the backing fabric and iron that onto the bow to seal them together. Sew up the two ends of the bow and fold to the centre of the back, securing with a small stitch. Finally, take the extra 3in (7.5cm) piece and fold round the centre of the bow, pulling tight to form the bow and stitch in place.

CHRISTMAS CARDS

These rustic cards (shown on page 110) are achieved by covering card mounts with hand-made paper and using rubber stamps on top. The designs are the bear and reindeer from the Animals of the North Sampler.

For both cards
◆ Two 3½ x 5in (9 x 13cm) pieces of 28 count linen in sand
◆ DMC stranded cottons from the main key
◆ Two 3½ x 5in (9 x 13cm) pieces of Vilene
◆ Two card mounts with 2¾ x 2¼in (7 x 5.8cm) apertures
◆ Sheet of red textured hand-made paper (from good art shops)
◆ Decorative rubber stamp with snowflake design
◆ Glue stick
◆ White acrylic or gouache paint

1 Find the centre of the fabric and begin stitching here over two threads of the linen following the main chart on page 109 and using two strands of stranded cotton for the cross stitch and one strand for the outlining, the backstitch and the star stitches (see Stitch Library page 125).

2 When the stitching is complete, press the work and iron Vilene onto the back.

To cover the card mount
1 Cut a piece of hand-made textured paper ½in (1cm) bigger all the way round than the card mount. Cover the card mount with glue, then press the card mount carefully and firmly down onto the hand-made paper and fold the paper in, mitring the corners and smoothing firmly.

2 To open the aperture, push the point of your scissors into the centre of the paper covering the aperture and cut a cross out to each corner. Fold the paper in neatly, trim, glue and press down.

3 When the glue has dried, mix the white paint with a little water and dip the rubber stamp into it and use to decorate the front of the card – it is best to practice this on a piece of scrap paper first.

4 Finally, mount the stitching into the card in the usual way (see Techniques page 126).

CANDLEFORD HALL SAMPLER

I have always derived a special enjoyment from being in old houses and I especially like the old black and white sixteenth-century buildings with their dark and musty rooms full of ghostly atmosphere. This sampler (shown on page 116) was inspired by visiting two of these old Halls just before Christmas when they were at their darkest and most romantic. I had also been reading about the technique of blackwork and this seemed the perfect subject for it. The distinctive architecture was evolving at the same time as ladies were covering fabric with the intricate black and white patterns of blackwork, or Spanish work as it was also known. I used a well-known strawberry pattern for the border and experimented with

Finished size: 9¾ x 12¼in (25 x 31cm)
Stitch count: 140 x 174

- ◆ **20 x 26in (51 x 66cm) 28 count Quaker cloth in grey**
- ◆ **DMC stranded cottons as listed in the key**
- ◆ **DMC thread, metallic silver**
- ◆ **Size 26 tapestry needle**
- ◆ **Gold-coloured charms – moon, bunch of keys and single key (optional)**
- ◆ **Mill Hill white seed beads**
- ◆ **White sewing cotton**
- ◆ **Beading needle**

1 Find the centre of the fabric and begin stitching here over two fabric threads following the chart on pages 114/115 and using an embroidery frame if you wish. Use two strands of stranded cotton for the cross stitch and one strand for the outlining, except for the following:

For the blackwork with white beads section use one strand for the backstitch and cross stitch.

For the small cross, apples, tree on the right, the book and the lighted window panes use one strand and backstitch.

For the trees on the left, the candle window, and the strawberry border use two strands for the backstitch and cross stitch.

For the stars use two strands and star stitch (see Stitch Library page 125).

For the candlestick use six strands of the light silver thread and cross stitch.

2 When the stitching is complete, sew on the charms if you are using them (positions indicated by black dots) or stitch the moon motif from the chart instead. Sew on the beads with white sewing cotton.

3 Finally, press the work carefully, avoiding the beads and charms, and frame (see Techniques page 125).

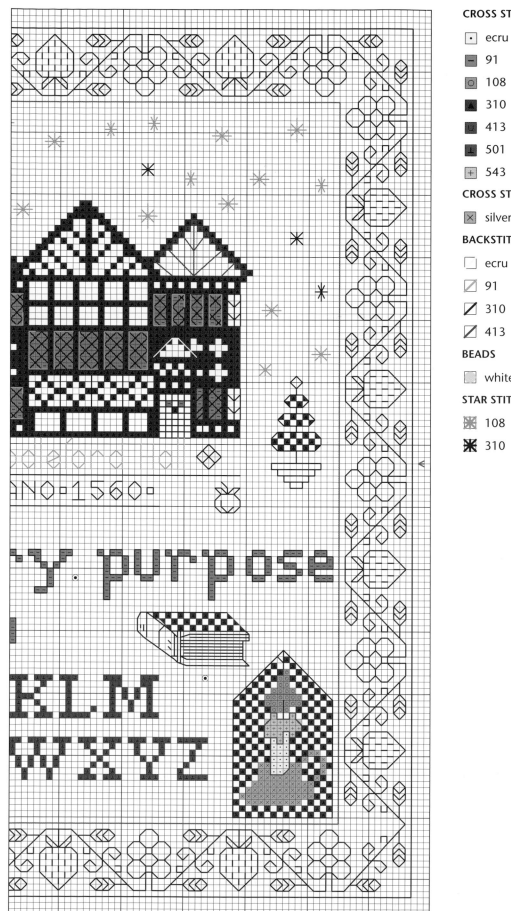

CROSS STITCH

·	ecru
▬	91
◎	108
▲	310
ᴜ	413
⊥	501
+	543

CROSS STITCH

✕	silver metallic

BACKSTITCH

☐	ecru
◺	91
◹	310
◺	413

BEADS

▨	white

STAR STITCH

✳	108
✹	310

CANDLEFORD HALL PAPERWEIGHT

This small project would make a lovely gift and the glass paperweight makes it extra special. The design makes good use of one of the topiary trees from the main Candleford Hall Sampler.

- ◆ **4in (10cm) square of 28 count Quaker cloth in grey**
- ◆ **DMC stranded cotton in black (310)**
- ◆ **4in (10cm) square of Vilene**
- ◆ **Glass paperweight for embroidery**
  (see Suppliers page 127)

1 Find the centre of the fabric and begin stitching here over two fabric threads following the main chart on pages 114/115 and using the photograph (left) as a guide to the design layout. Use one strand of stranded cotton throughout and a flexihoop if you wish.

2 When the stitching is complete, press the work and iron Vilene onto the back according to the manufacturer's instructions.

3 Finally, trim the design and mount in the paperweight according to the manufacturer's instructions.

The dramatic Candleford Hall Sampler and its spin-off projects – a paperweight, bookmark and key keeper – all using blackwork to great effect

CANDLEFORD HALL KEY KEEPER

This small design (shown on page 117) has its own chart (below). It was intended to mimic an antique and to look attractive attached to an old ornate key or hanging from an old bureau for decoration.

◆ Two 3in (7.5cm) squares of 32 count Belfast raw linen
◆ DMC stranded cotton in black (310)
◆ 15in (38cm) length of twisted cord in black and white stranded cotton
◆ Small gold key charm (optional)
◆ Small amount of polyester wadding
◆ Four pearl-headed pins

1 Find the centre of one square of linen and begin stitching over two fabric threads following the chart below, using one strand of DMC black (310) stranded cotton for all the backstitch. Use a flexihoop if you wish.

2 When the stitching is complete, use matching thread to sew on the key charm if you are using it.

3 Take the second square of linen and place it right sides together with the embroidered piece. Stitch round three sides ¼in (5mm) from the design, then trim the edges, clip the corners and turn right side out. Stuff with polyester wadding and sew up the fourth side.

4 Make the twisted cord from black and white stranded cotton (see Techniques page 126) and sew it all the way round the key keeper, making a loop at the top left-hand corner and finally pushing the pearl-headed pins into the corners.

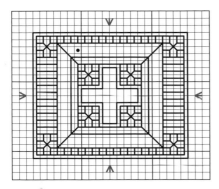

CANDLEFORD HALL BOOKMARK

This elegant bookmark (see page 116) uses a section of the blackwork border pattern from the main Candleford Hall Sampler. The simple blackwork lines in this segment create a flowing pattern that would work well as a border to a small picture, perhaps worked around the house or candle motif from the main sampler. The blackwork for the bookmark could also be stitched in a different colour: for example, red against a cream fabric would look very effective.

◆ 7 x 3in (18 x 7.5cm) 28 count Quaker cloth in grey
◆ DMC stranded cotton in black (310)
◆ 7 x 3in (18 x 7.5cm) piece of Vilene
◆ Ready-made bookmark card mount (see Suppliers page 127)

1 Find the centre of the fabric and begin stitching here over two threads following the chart on pages 114/115 and with reference to the photograph on page 116. Use two strands of stranded cotton throughout for the backstitch.

2 When the stitching is complete, press the work and iron the piece of Vilene onto the back.

3 Finally, trim the embroidery to fit the purchased bookmark and mount according to the manufacturer's instructions.

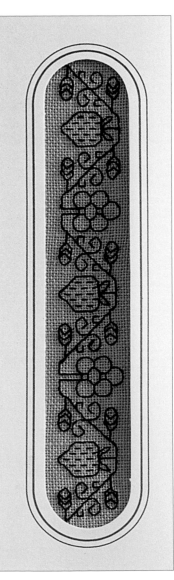

LETTERING LIBRARY

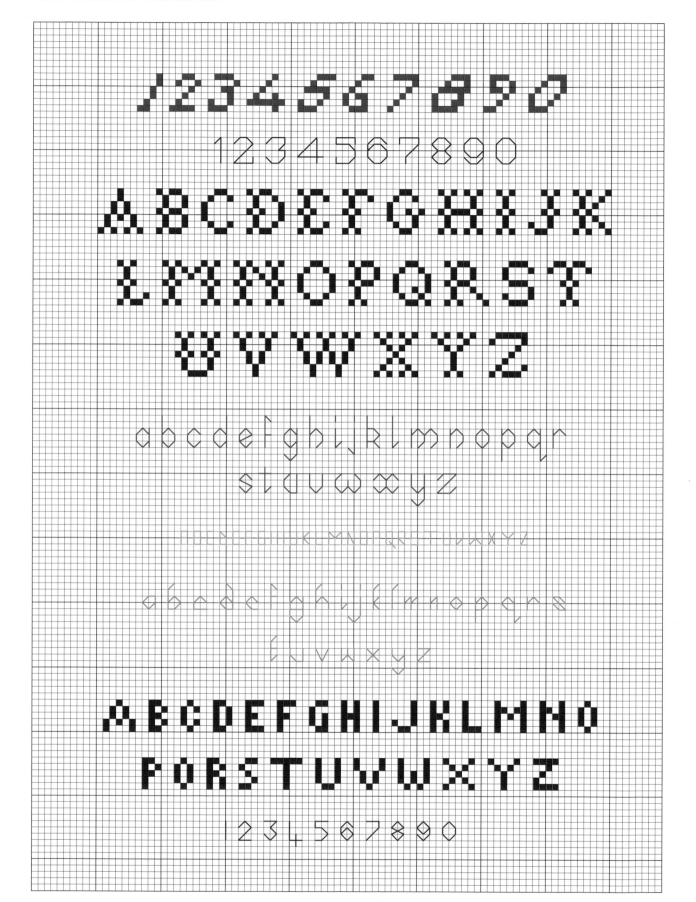

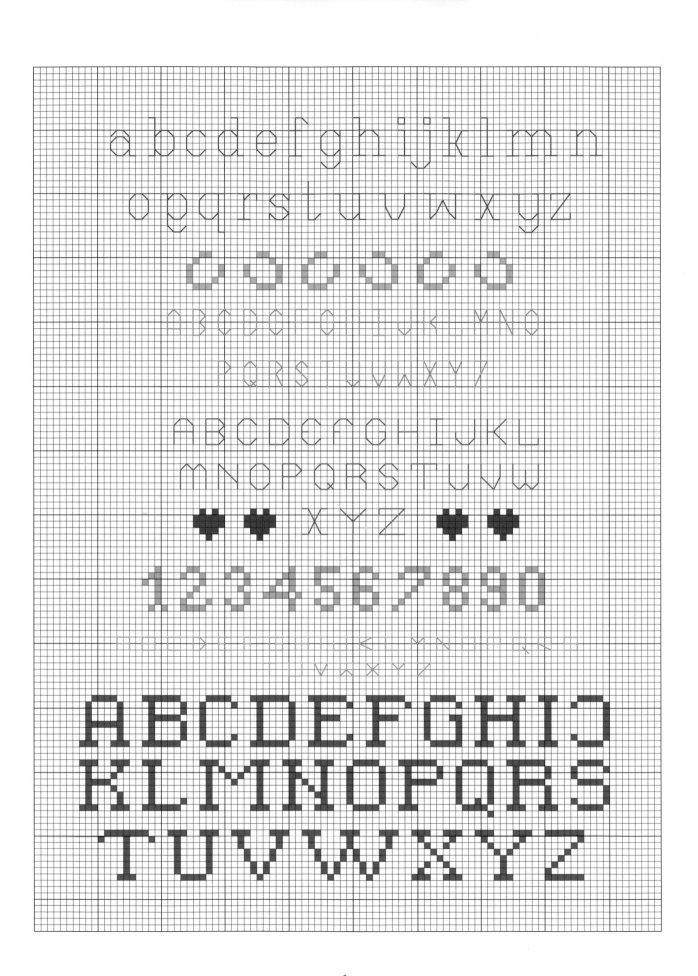

BEST WISHES

FOR YOUR ANNIVERSARY

HAPPY BIRTHDAY

on our anniversary

with love

Happy Easter

with love at Thanksgiving

WELCOME

New Home

GOOD LUCK

GET WELL

Mother's Day   Father's Day

Happy Christmas

Season's Greetings

with love

TEMPLATES

Templates A to G are used in the Winter's Tale spin-off projects on pages 96–99. Trace the shapes carefully onto thin card and cut out, marking each with its relevant letter for easy identification.

STITCH LIBRARY

Starting and Finishing

To start off your first length of thread, make a knot at one end and push the needle through to the back of the fabric, about 1¼in (3cm) from your starting point, leaving the knot on the right side. Stitch towards the knot, securing the thread at the back of the fabric as you go. When the thread is secure, cut off the knot.

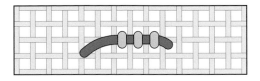

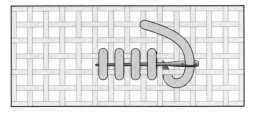

To finish off a thread or start new threads, simply weave the thread into the back of several worked stitches and then trim off neatly.

Algerian Eye Stitch

This pretty star-shaped stitch can be used with cross stitch to great effect. It generally occupies the space of

two cross stitches and is worked in such a way that an evenly shaped, almost square stitch is produced with a small hole formed in the centre.

Antique Hemstitch

To work this stitch, decide where the edge of the hem will come and withdraw two or three threads along

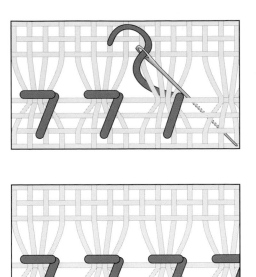

the length of the piece. Fold the hem so that the turned-under edge just touches the drawn threads and tack in place. Beginning at the left-hand end of the wrong side, bring the thread through from inside the hem, emerging on the wrong side three threads down from the drawn area. Move the needle two threads to the right and surround four of the threads (see diagram above). Bring the needle back to the right of the clump of threads and insert it between the hem and the front of the fabric, emerging two threads to the right, ready to take another stitch. Pull the thread tight enough to pull the group of threads together, then repeat.

Backstitch and Outlining

Backstitch is indicated on charts by a solid coloured line. It is worked on its own or on top of stitches for detail and as an outline around areas of completed cross stitches to add definition.

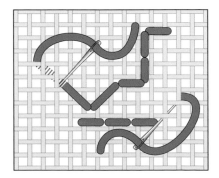

To work backstitch, pull the needle through the hole in the fabric at 1 (see diagram on page 123), then push back through at 2. Pull the needle through at 3, push to the back at 1, then repeat the process to make the next stitch. This produces short stitches at the front of the work and longer ones at the back.

Blanket Stitch

This is a variable and useful stitch. Bring the thread out on the lower line shown in the diagram below. Re-insert the needle at 1 on the upper line and out again at 2, with the thread under the needle point so a loop is formed.

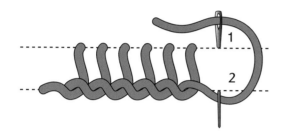

Cross Stitch

Each coloured square on the chart represents one complete cross stitch. The cross stitches in this book are generally worked over two threads of linen or one block of Aida fabric unless otherwise stated. A cross

Cross stitch on Aida

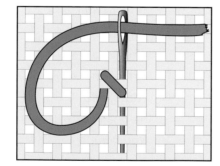

Cross stitch on evenweave

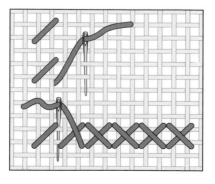

stitch is worked in two stages: a diagonal stitch is worked over two threads (or one block), then a second diagonal stitch is worked over the first stitch, but in the opposite direction to form a cross. If you have a large area to cover, work a row of half cross stitches in one direction and then work back in the opposite direction with diagonal stitches to complete each cross. The upper stitches of all the crosses should lie in the same direction to produce a neat effect.

French Knot

A French knot is a useful little stitch and may be used in addition to cross stitch to add texture and emphasis.

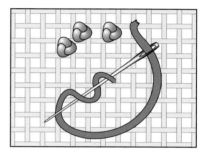

To work, bring the needle up to the right side of the fabric, hold the thread down with the left thumb and wind the thread around the needle twice. Still holding the thread taut, put the needle through to the back of the work, one thread or part of a block away from the entry point. If you want bigger knots, add more thread to the needle as this produces a better effect than winding more times.

Half Cross Stitch

This is simply one half of a cross stitch, with the diagonal facing the same way as the upper stitches of each complete cross stitch.

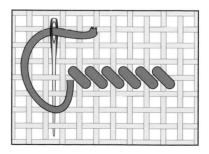

Quilting Stitch

This is basically a small, neat running stitch, with the thread being passed under and over the fabric with regular spacing.

Star Stitch

This stitch is rather similar to Algerian eye stitch but can be made over any number of threads and so can be almost any size.

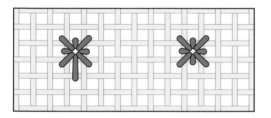

Whipped Backstitch

This is a useful and decorative embellishment to backstitch. First stitch the line or area of backstitch in the normal way, over two threads of linen or one block of Aida. Change the colour of the thread in your needle and 'whip' or stitch around each backstitch without piercing the fabric, as shown in the diagram.

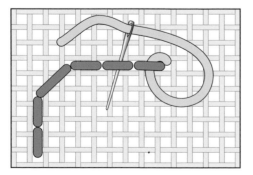

TECHNIQUES

Washing and Ironing Embroidery

If it becomes necessary to wash a piece of stitching, make sure it is colourfast first. Wash with bleach-free soap in hand-hot water. Squeeze gently but never rub or wring. Rinse in plenty of cold or lukewarm water and dry naturally.

To iron cross stitch, use a hot setting on a steam iron and cover the ironing board with a thick layer of towelling. Place the stitching on this, right side down, and press the fabric firmly, avoiding any charms, buttons or metallic threads used.

Mounting and Framing Embroidery

It is best to take large samplers and pictures to a professional framer, who will be able to lace and stretch the fabric correctly and cut any surrounding mounts accurately. If mounting work yourself, use acid-free mounting board in a colour that will not show through the embroidery. Cut the mounting board to fit inside your picture frame and allowing for the thickness of the fabric pulled over the edges of the board. There are two common methods used for mounting – taping and lacing.

Taping method

Place the cut board on the reverse of the work in the position required. Starting from the centre of one of the longest edges, fold the fabric over the board and pin through the fabric into the edge of the board to keep the fabric from moving. Check it is in the correct place with no wrinkles or bumps. Stick the work in place using strips of double-sided adhesive tape, removing the pins once finished (see diagram).

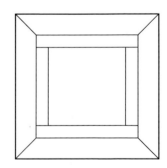

Taping method

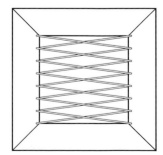

Lacing method

Lacing method

Pin the work in place on the board as above, then working from the centre and using very long lengths of very strong thread, lace backwards and forwards across the gap (see diagram on page 125). Remove the pins. Repeat this process for the shorter sides, taking care to mitre or fold the corners in neatly.

If mounting work into commercial products, such as paperweights or trinket box lids, follow the manufacturer's instructions. For small pieces of work back with lightweight iron-on interfacing to prevent the fabric wrinkling, and then mount.

Using Iron-on Interfacing and Bondaweb

Iron-on interfacing such as that made by Vilene is very useful when mounting pieces in small objects. It fuses with and strengthens the fabric, stabilises the stitches, helps to make cutting the embroidery to size easier and stops cut edges fraying. Bondaweb, also made by Vilene, is a soft web impregnated with adhesive making it ideal for attaching one fabric to another.

To apply interfacing cut a piece roughly to the size required and place it shiny side down on the back of the embroidery. Using an iron on medium heat, press into a thick, fluffy towel for fifteen to twenty seconds. Try peeling the interfacing away from one of the corners – if it peels hold the hot iron over it a little longer until it is securely glued. Trim the work as necessary.

To apply Bondaweb, cut a piece roughly to the size required and using a dry iron place it adhesive side downwards onto the wrong side of the fabric. Draw and cut out the shape required and peel off the paper backing. Place the shape onto your main fabric, right side up, cover with a damp cloth and press with a hot, dry iron. Leave to cool.

Mounting Embroidery in a Card or Tag

Ready-made card mounts are pre-folded and have three sections, the middle one having a window for your embroidery.

First make sure your embroidery looks good in the window space, then trim your design to the correct

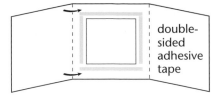

size. Put small lengths of double-sided adhesive tape around the window area and remove the backing from the tape. Lay the card on top of the embroidery so that it shows neatly through the window. Press into place. Fold the third of the card to cover the back of the embroidery, ensuring that the card opens correctly before securing with double-sided adhesive tape.

Making a Twisted Cord

Many designs are beautifully finished off by the addition of a twisted cord that reflects the colours used in the embroidery. Success in making an even and tightly twisted cord depends on keeping the threads taut at all times.

Cut the required number of lengths of stranded cotton – as a rough guide this length must be 2½ to 3 times longer than the finished length required. Knot the lengths together at one end and loop this around a door handle or ask a friend to hold it. Knot the other ends of the strands together and pass a pencil through the loop. Keeping the thread taut, wind the pencil round and round so that the thread twists, eventually coiling around itself. Carefully bring the two knotted ends together so that both halves of the thread twist around one another. Gently pull and ease the cord until it is evenly twisted then knot the ends together to prevent them from unravelling. Trim the ends beyond the knots. If required you can leave about ⅜in (1cm) beyond the knots and tease these out with a pin to make mini tassels. To make a two- or three-colour twisted cord, simply start with groups of different coloured thread of the required length bunched together.

SUPPLIERS

When contacting suppliers by post, remember to use a stamped self-addressed envelope.

The Voirrey Embroidery Centre

Brimstage Hall, Wirral L63 6JA

Tel: 0151 342 3514 Fax: 0151 3425161

For linen, evenweave, threads, beads, plastic canvas and many other supplies

Willow Fabrics

27 Willow Green, Knutsford WA16 6AX

Tel: 0156562 1098; Fax: 01565 653233

For fabrics, Caron threads, beads and many other supplies

Framecraft

372–376 Summer Lane

Hockley, Birmingham B19 3QA

Tel: 0121 212 0551; Fax: 0121 212 0552

For Mill Hill buttons, charms, ready-made items like boxes, pincushions, spoons, bookmarks, napkin holders, cards, trinket pots etc. Many of the charms used came from 'Creative Beginnings' available through Framecraft or good local retailers

The Quilt Room

20 West Street, Dorking, Surrey RH4 1BL

Tel: 01306 740739 (shop) 01306 877307 (mail order)

Fax: 01306 877407

For American cotton fabric in current designs, Debbie Mumm buttons and all quilting supplies

Calico Gift Shop

32a Grange Road, West Kirby, Wirral L48 4EF

Tel: 0151 6254434

For garden picture frames 'Two's Company' and other small picture frames

John Lewis

(Branches in many towns and cities)

For general haberdashery, decorated ribbons, tea towels, towels, lace, trimmings etc.

ACKNOWLEDGEMENTS

I would like to thank all my family, especially my husband David and daughters Sarah and Rosie for all their support and encouragement. Thanks to everyone at David & Charles and particularly Cheryl Brown, Lin Clements, Brenda Morrison, and Lucy Kind for their skills and enthusiasm in bringing this book about. Thanks to Rebecca Bradshaw for encouraging me to design for cross stitch, to Candae Connor, now back in the States, for her inspiration and friendship, and to Rod Holmes for collecting quotations for me to stitch. Thanks to all the helpful and knowledgeable ladies at the Voirrey Embroidery Centre, to Susan and Martin Penny for their excellent charts and to David Johnson for the wonderful photography.

INDEX